MY STORY OF A SHARECROPPER'S LIFE

Made History at Death as America's oldest Man

Lived in Three Centuries

JIM MCKNIGHT

Retired Business & Economic Community
Development Consultant

SAHARA BOWSER

Author & Genealogist

Holliday/Mc Fadden Family Tree

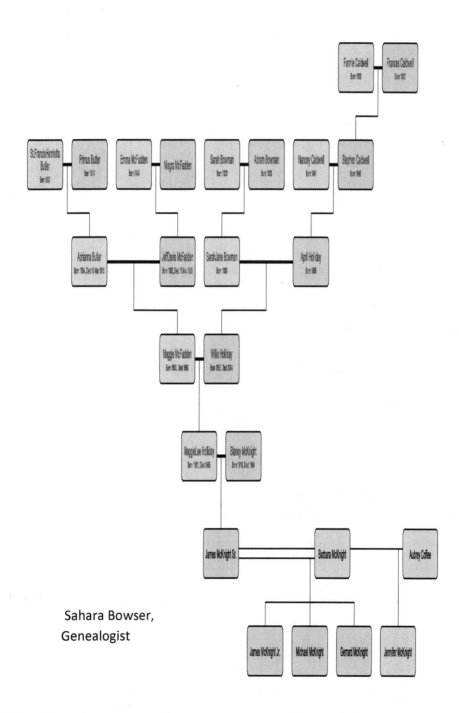

Sahara Bowser,
Genealogist

"In all of us there is a hunger, marrow deep, to know our heritage, to know who we are and where we came from".

--Alex Haley

Contents

ACKNOWLEDGMENTS

Big thank you to family and friends of Willie Holliday Sr., for allowing me to recreate an ancestral story of your father and grandfather, Willie Holliday Sr. It was a pleasure meeting and interviewing you for "My Story of the Sharecropper's Life".

This story reflects an important part of your heritage and one that I hope you will cherish and appreciate always. The purpose of separating Africans Americans during slavery was to prevent them from ever knowing family members. Despite the odds, I have successfully traced your ancestry back to 1810.

Working on this project was special to me not only because Willie Holliday Sr. was impressive man but also because I, too, have roots in South Carolina and my ancestor's lives were similar.

I thank all of you for making this book possible. Special thanks to those who took the time to meet with me and give interviews and contribute family details. Big thank you to Cynthia and George McDaniel—Willie Holliday's grand-daughter and grandson-in-law. Your photos, input, and ongoing support is greatly appreciated. Thank you Mrs. Dorothy Conyers, Willie Holliday's youngest daughter. You have been a blessing to this book.

I was honored to meet with Rev. W.T. Johnson, pastor of the Taw Caw Baptist Church in Summerton, S.C. Big thank you Rev. Johnson for sharing many wonderful stories and memories. Special thanks to Rev. Willie Robinson, grandson of Willie Holliday Sr. for sharing stories and memories. I would like to thank Mr. John Evans Carter for sharing intimate memories of his friendship with Willie Holliday as fellow Deacon and Mason. Many thanks to Karl Holliday and his wife for "going the extra mile".

Lastly, big thank you to Mrs. Odessa Holliday, 89 years young. It was a joy meeting with you at your home in Philly and talking about the good old days.

To the young descendants of Willie Holliday Sr. may this book be your legacy to learn from the past and build for the future.

Thanks to the following family members and friends:

Alex Payne (Great-great grandson)

Leasia McKnight (Great-great granddaughter)

Aaron Holliday (Grandson)

Michela McKnight (Great-great granddaughter)

Johnnie E. Holliday (Grandson)

Michael McKnight (Great-grandson)

Bert Shuler Johnson (relative)

Esther Carter (neighbor)

Sonny Richburg (neighbor)

Leanese "Sank" Shuler (Daughter)

Ben Holliday (Grandson)

Arnie Smaw (Grandson)

James McKnight Jr. (Great-grandson)

Gerard McKnight (Great-grandson)

Jenn McKnight (Great-granddaughter)

Rodney Holliday (Grandson)

J. R. Speed

Last but not least, Thank you Brother Joseph Jones Jr.

Note from Author/Genealogist Sahara Bowser

Willie Holliday Sr., was born before birthdays were officially registered. Babies were birthed at home and it was up to families to maintain accurate records.

Consequently, United States census records are often inconsistent and inaccurate. Census accuracy depends on the informant's knowledge and the enumerator's diligence, both which can vary and produce frequent conflicts in census information.

The 1900 U.S. Census listing Willie Holliday's birth year as 1895 is one such discrepancy. Genealogy research shows this date to be incorrect. The principal events used to arrive at a more accurate birthday for Willie Holliday Sr. were the death certificates of two of Willie's siblings, Elie Holliday & Estelle Holliday Garris.

Elie Holliday's death certificate lists his birth year as 1895, and Willie was older than Elie. In addition, Estelle's death certificate lists her birth year as 1889 and not 1881 as recorded on the 1900 U.S. Census. It appears that on the 1900 U.S. Census the children's birth years were off by two years. Since Willie is older than Elie but younger than Estelle, Willie Holliday Sr.'s year of birth had to be between 1892 and 1893. The death certificates on Willie's siblings are reliable documents since they were recorded when record keeping was mandated by the State.

Willie Holliday Sr. believed his birth year to be 1893. Therefore, from a genealogy standpoint, when all principal events are weighed in, Willie Holliday, Sr., age at death was between 111 and 112.

Deacon Willie Holliday's Special Scripture and his signature, taken from his personal copy of Star Book for Ministers.

Willie Holliday Sr., holding copy of Star Book for Ministers

CHAPTER 1

THE MAN WHO LIVED IN THREE CENTURIES

Willie Holliday Sr., was officially a centenarian.

On November 17, 1993, Willie Holliday Sr., turned 100 years old. Reaching the triple digits is an accomplishment in itself, but Mr. Holliday would also have the distinction of living in three centuries which is even rarer, the 1800s, 1900s, and the 2000s.

What had Mr. Holliday done to live so long everyone asked? Did he have a lifestyle secret to share, or was he just blessed with a longevity gene? Mr. Holliday didn't know why he had lived so long. He believed he was blessed, certainly, but beyond that he had just lived his life believing in God, hard work, and getting a good night's rest. However, one thing he knew for sure, his longevity didn't stem from living an easy life because by no means was his life easy.

Willie Holliday Sr., had lived through some of the worst hard times. If he could contribute his longevity to anything it was his steadfast faith in God which allowed him to triumph over adversity without letting it triumph over him. Maybe, just maybe, that was the secret.

As birthday greetings came in from the White House and the Governor's office, family members gathered around the patriarch in celebration and joy. All of Willie Sr.'s surviving children were there, many of his grandchildren, some great-grandchildren, and even a few great-great-grandchildren. In addition, in attendance were his siblings, cousins, nieces, nephews, other relatives, friends, and fellow Masons from Lodge #99. This was more than a birthday celebration. It was also a celebration of family, of overcoming, of strength, and of love. It was a day to look back at the life of a father who had been the rock, anchor, and mortar that held the family together.

Loud chatter and laughter filled the room. Adding ambiance to the occasion were the colorful balloons and festive streamers lining the walls.

Soon small talk turned to stories of the past. Everyone had a "hard times" story to tell. laugh about hard times now but they weren't so funny back then.

You can't talk about the past without talking about the hard times, "because the only times we had were hard times", someone made a joke. But it was true. The Hollidays had grown up on the rough side of the mountain. They could The beautiful vibes and strong synchronicity made Willie Holliday Sr. proud. He loved when the family got along good because Lords knows they didn't always see eye to eye. As in all families there were those you love to see come and love to see go. However, just for tonight all differences were put aside and everyone was laughing together and enjoying the good home cooked food. One thing was for sure, no matter how good or bad the old days were, you can't bring them back and wouldn't want to anyway.

Willie Holliday Sr., looked every bit the elder statesman. He was impeccably dressed in a white full length tuxedo with white silk lapels and tails. Completing his outfit were a white silk shirt, cummerbund and bow tie. Willie Holliday strolled into the party walking with a cane. He didn't need help walking, it just added to his elegance. "I am dressing up like I am going to get married", he joked. Willie Sr., always enjoyed a good laugh. "Worry-ation will kill you", he like to say. Willie Sr. said a lot of things, some funny and some serious. Call them "Willie Holliday's nuggets" or whatever, but when he started rapping you had better take heed. He got up every morning praising Jesus and giving thanks. "If you don't have but a little you should still give thanks. You will get by."

A money hat stacked with dollar bills set regally on Willie Holliday's head and another money tree set on the table beside him. He wore the money hat proudly, smiling as a photo was snapped of him with his long fingers folded across his white silk vest. The money trees were "probably more money than he made in a lifetime of sharecropping", someone joked. Everybody laughed at that and Mr. Holliday laughed right along with them. He was in good spirits. He introduced the family to his "girl friend", who was actually his nurse, a young woman named Hattie. Mr. Holliday had a crush on Hattie. He didn't want Nurse Hattie to take care of any other patients.

It is a fact that you can tell a tree's worthiness by the fruit that it bears and the descendants of Willie Holliday Sr., had done him proud. The family included many college graduates working in a variety of professions—engineers, medical doctors, entrepreneurs, marketing, businesspeople, military veterans, government and religious figures.

Willie Holliday Sr.'s life had revolved around God, farming, and family. He was the father of ten children plus one, a grandson, whom he raised. When it comes to family memories, each child remembers things differently, but grandson Jim McKnight or "Boy", as he was affectionately called, surely spoke for all when he reiterated that his grandfather "instilled principles, morals, values, and character in all of his children. Education was important as were the responsibilities on the farm".[1] Indeed, farming was very important to Willie Holliday Sr., because for 59 years, nearly half of his life, he was a sharecropper.

Booker T. Washington said it best, "No race can prosper till it learns that there is as much dignity in tilling a field as in writing a poem".

And this was the dignity in which Willie Holliday Sr., embraced sharecropping. He wasn't just a sharecropper but an entrepreneur who ran a business that happens to be sharecropping. His extensive knowledge of agriculture and farm management was equivalent to a college degree. Despite the economic injustices of sharecropping, Willie Sr. was innovative in finding ways to keep his family fed and still meet his financial obligations to his creditors. More importantly, he managed this with little formal education and in one of the most racist states in America.

Heretofore they would gather together to celebrate one birthday after another because Willie Holliday Sr. wasn't done yet. For the remainder of the 1990s and on into the new millennium, The Holliday family never imagine they would be celebrating their beloved patriarch's 100th Birthday as no other family member had lived that long. Nor could they imagine that he would reach one milestone birthday after another before reaching super-centenarian status and dying on December 19, 2004, at 112 ½ years old, the oldest man in South Carolina and one of very few to live in three centuries.

HOLLIDAY FAMILY GATHER FOR
109TH BIRTHDAY CELEBRATION

CHAPTER 2

HUMBLE BEGINNINGS

Willie Holliday, Sr., was born on November 17, 1893, in the Davis Station community of Summerton, South Carolina, located in Clarendon County. Willie's parents, April and Sarah Jane (Bowman) Holliday, had decided on the name Willie if the baby was a boy, Willie G. to be exact. It is unknown what the G stood for because Willie never used it and soon it disappeared from his name. Sarah Jane held little Willie close to her heart and prayed he would grow

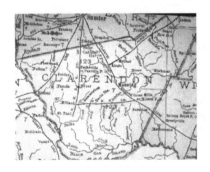

big and strong. Sarah Jane knew the pain of losing a child as she had lost two babies in a row. Child mortality rates were high for sharecropper's children because of squalid conditions and inadequate diets. Infants were susceptible to gastro-intestinal diseases and older children died from respiratory illnesses like whooping cough and influenza.

The house the Hollidays called home was the typical sharecropper's shack with peeling paint and a leaky roof. As the Fall temperatures chilled into Winter, the farm house became downright chilly. The holes in the depilated wooden walls were plugged up with rags but strong winds still found their way inside. Sarah Jane swaddled up little Willie and took him to meet his brother and sister; five-year-old Epherm and four-year-old Estelle.

The children played on the cold dirt floor waiting for mama to come and make them spoon bread breakfast.

November was laying by and gathering time for April Holliday, a sharecropper, who was out working in the cotton fields when word reached him that Sarah Jane had delivered a baby boy. April threw his old slouch hat in the air and caught it on his brogan shoe, ecstatic and overjoyed to have another son. April lived the hardscrabble life of a sharecropper and could use extra pairs of hands on the farm. His cotton crop hadn't done too good this season and April feared he wasn't going to reap much of a return on his labor after the land owner deducted for this and that. Which meant he would have to borrow against next year's profits to make ends meet, same as he had done last year and the year before that.

April was a smart man who could read, write, and do arithmetic, and he was very much aware of the cycle of debt he had gotten himself into.

April didn't like admitting he was frustrated but he was. The land owner wanted cotton, cotton, and more cotton; so much cotton that April had no time to grow anything else. The family needed vegetables to supplement their meager fare of cornbread, fatback, pork, and molasses. As it was, April had to depend on Sarah Jane to plant and grow vegetables because he had no time. Sarah Jane was doing a good job considering she was also keeping house and taking care of the children. Sarah Jane had been able to grow and can enough vegetables to get them through the winter months. Keeping a vegetable garden would become Sarah Jane's passion.

April (Caldwell) Holliday

April (Caldwell) Holliday was born enslaved in Clarendon County, South Carolina in 1859, three years before the Emancipation. April was too young to remember being in bondage. His parents were named Stephen and Nancey Caldwell and he had a sister two years older named Lanarie.

Stephen, age 30, and Nancey, age 28, had settled in Davis Station after the Civil War and were trying to blend into society as freed people.[2] Davis Station was the swamp area of Summerton around nearby Jordan and Potato Creek. African Americans had lived in Davis Station since slavery times when Summerton was called

"Summer Town" where the wealthy plantation owners relocated during the summer to escape what was believed to be malaria-carrying mosquitos in the swamp areas.

In 1889, "Summer Town" was officially legislated a town and its name changed to Summerton.

Caldwell Household 1870 Census

Clarendon County wasn't such a bad place for newly freed African Americans. The Fifteenth Amendment of the Constitution had given citizens of every "race, color, or previous condition of servitude" the right to vote and J. D. Warley, a black minister and farmer from Clarendon county, had been elected to the House of Representative. Warley represented Clarendon County as a Congressman from 1870-1874 and as a Senator from 1874-1877.

He was also active in the Republican party serving as election commissioner, magistrate, trial justice, and chairman of the Clarendon County Republican.

Stephen Caldwell was a sharecropper, one of few livelihoods available to former slaves. Tenant farmer and farm hand were other possibilities. Sharecropping was a form of agriculture that had started in sixteenth century Europe but the Emancipation of slaves gave it new life. Newly freed African Americans needed work and a place to live and former slaveholders needed someone to farm the land left abandoned after slavery. It was a match made in hell for freed people who were exploited and ripped off in the process.

Stephen Caldwell was a skilled carpenter, a very valuable trade during slavery. The plantation system relied heavily on slave craftsmen in the colonial world where everything was made of wood, therefore, black carpenters were very high in demand. [3] Practically everything in the colonial South was built by free and enslaved carpenters. In fact, it was enslaved and free black men who help build the White House. Copies of payroll documents from the project show the amount of pay earned by slaves with first names like Tom, Peter, and Ben. Their pay went directly to their slaveholder.

Unfortunately, after the Civil War Stephen Caldwell's carpentry skills were no longer in demand and he had no choice but to turn to sharecropping to make ends meet. In addition, carpentry and other crafts were becoming more formalize, requiring schooling, if not licenses. The

Freedman's Bureau founded Hampton Institute to train African Americans in carpentry which became a model for Booker T. Washington's Tuskegee Institute.

Despite the dire circumstances Stephen found himself in, he did not lose his love for carpentry. In fact, he would take one of his grandsons under his wing and teach him the trade in a sort of apprenticeship and the grandson would love carpentry as much as Stephen did. That grandson was Willie Holliday Sr. When Willie was around age 15, him and Granddad Steve started a carpentry business and earned pretty good money doing carpentry jobs around Clarendon County. Willie prided himself on being a carpenter. He developed skills in manual dexterity and mathematical aptitude. Willie's grandfather and father could read, write, and do figures, and were good role models for little Willie.

The Caldwells were a large extended family. According to the USDA Agricultural records, Stephen rented 30 acres of land and had 15 cows.[4] April's Grandparents, Frances and Fannie Caldwell lived in a separate house on the land and helped with farming. They were Frances born in 1812 and Fannie in 1810. At the end of the Civil War the couple was in their late 50s and had spent half of their lives enslaved. Frances and Fannie's younger son Jacob (Jake), age 28, lived on a smaller farm of 5 acres with his wife Lizzie and three little girls, Fannie (named for her grandmother), Rina and Susan. Frances' brother, Lenalich, 56 years old, also lived nearby with his wife Sukey. Lenalich had a 22-year-old, Lemrick, and Lemrick and his wife had two sons, Paris and Lemrick Jr.

The Caldwells appear close knit and had each other's back. Therefore, it is surprising that by the 1880 U.S. Census April Caldwell was no longer using the surname Caldwell but was now April Holliday.

- On the U.S. Census 1870 Stephen Caldwell and Nancey Caldwell were the parents of April Caldwell.
- On the U.S. Census 1880 Stephen Caldwell and Nancey Caldwell are the parents of April Holliday.

The reason April changed his surname is unknown, however, this wasn't uncommon to do among freed people.

After slavery African Americans did not have surnames and there were no rules in place for choosing one. When comparing the 1860 Census with the 1870 Census, it appears most former slaves took the surnames of slaveholders in Clarendon County; for example, Holladay, Briggs, Dingle, Harvin, Johnson, McFadden, Davis, McDonald, Livingston, Manning, Montgomery, Richardson, McKnight, all slaveholders' names.

The State of South Carolina did not register births until 1915, therefore, surnames could be changed at will. It wasn't unusual for members of the same family to chose different surnames or the same name with a variation in the spelling.

Despite the ambiguities of the name change, April Caldwell was heretofore April Holliday. In a similar case, co-author of this book, Jim McKnight, was called "Boy Holliday" and lived under the last name Holliday until age sixteen when he moved to New Jersey with his parents. Also, Willie Holliday's son Edward spells his surname with a variation of Holliday—Holiday minus an 'L'.

Acclimating into the dominant culture presented many challenges and choosing surnames was an insignificant phenomenon compared to other dilemmas faced by the Caldwells and other newly freed African Americans. It was a struggle carving out a new life as freed people especially for older people like Frances and Fannie Caldwell. They questioned the concept of freedom because under slavery you worked for nothing and as freed people working as sharecroppers, they were still working for nothing. They question if freedom was a blessing or a curse?

.

Sarah Bowman-Holliday

Willie Holliday Sr.'s mother, Sarah Jane Bowman was born in 1866 to Abram and Sarah Bowman. The family lived in St. Paul Township, Clarendon County, South Carolina. Sarah was the youngest of six children and was named for her mother.[5]

Sarah Jane's father, Abram, served with the Army's USCT during the Civil War. 5000 black troops from South Carolina volunteered and fought and Abram Bowman was one of them.

[5] United States Census, 1870," database with images, FamilySearch (https://familysearch.org/ark:/61903/1:1:M8R8-RBJ: 12 April 2016), Sarah J Bowman in household of Abram Bowman, South Carolina, United States;

slaves built confederate forts and made artillery. Female slaves cooked for the Confederate army and nursed wounded soldiers. Two years into the war, the North was losing badly, therefore, freeing the slaves was a strategic way in taking away the South's advantage. After Lincoln signed the Emancipation Proclamation into law, thousands of southern black men enlisted in the Union Army, including Willie Holliday's grandfather, Abram Bowman.

Army Private Abram Bowman enlisted in October, 1864, at age 45. Abram was assigned to the U.S. Colored Troops (USCT) in Heavy Artillery. The USCT was an army unit set up specifically for African Americans because they were not allowed to fight alongside whites. After the Civil War, the USCT was disbanded but because of its exemplary performance the Army decided to establish Black Calvary and Infantry regiments which were made up of predominantly USCT veterans. The USCT veterans later became known as the "Buffalo Soldiers".

April & Sarah Jane Holliday

After a brief courtship, April and Sarah Jane married in 1887. Willie was the third of nine children born to the couple, six boys and three girls. The children are:

- Epherm - September 25, 1888 – June 1972
- Estelle (Garris) - 1889 – December 14, 1937
- Willie G.   - November 17, 1893 – December 19, 2004
- Robert Elie - September 27, 1895 – March 5, 1961
- Richard   - March 1899 - unknown
- Rebecca (Rembert) - May 8, 1900 – August 18, 1992

- John Elliott - October 4, 1904 – December 18, 1991

- Blany - March 23, 1906 – 1972

- Naomi (Stokes) - July 12, 1908 – February 23, 2007

April and Sarah Jane instilled in their children the love of God, family, and work. Willie Holliday exemplified these early teachings throughout his life. Willie maintained strong Christian beliefs, a sound work ethic, and love and respect for family. As a child he was required to teach, protect, and set good examples for his younger brothers and sisters. Willie Holliday's youngest sister, Naomi Stokes, remembers a list of Willie's values which are: You should obey God's laws, obey your parents, be kind to one another, and pray for those who mistreat you."[6]

One of Willie's chores was babysitting the younger children, a chore he despised because it got in the way of his playing time. Playing time was precious to children of Willie's era because they got very little. Children were required to work and help out their parents. Willie's strategy was getting the infants to sleep as quickly as possible thereby gaining more playing time.

April Holliday was a strong father figure who helped shaped Willie's character by teaching him responsibility at an early age. Willie began helping his father on the farm at around age five or six. Willie was a quick learner and picked up vital farming skills that he would rely on later in adulthood. Willie was a big help to his father on the the farm, but his ~~real interest was carpentry,~~ a trade he learned from his ~~grandfather, Stephen.~~ Toiling and Thanking God Fills a Long Life. The State Newspaper. July 13, 2004, 2.

Stephen was a skilled carpenter and Willie acted as an apprentice to Stephen, becoming a skilled carpenter by the time he was in his teens. The 1910 U.S. Census records show Willie and granddad Stephen earning wages doing carpentry jobs.

CHAPTER 3

TAW CAW MISSIONARY BAPTIST CHURCH

Taw Caw Missionary Baptist Church, Summerton, S.C.

The Hollidays attended Taw Caw Missionary Baptist Church, one of the oldest black churches in South Carolina, located in Summerton, S.C. Bible reading and scripture study was a big part of family life in the Holliday household. After slavery African Americans did not have a church building to worship in so many continue worshipping the Lord the way they had done during slavery, under a "Brush Arbor", sometimes referred to as "Bush Arbor". During slavery blacks were forbidden to gather in groups and stole away to secret places like clinging shade trees where they could conceal themselves.

In 1886, the white owners of the Taw Caw Church sold the building and land to the black worshippers for $400.00, a magnificent sum at that time. The church building dated back to 1859 and in addition to paying the sales price, many renovations have had to be made. Taw Caw members made a number of sacrifices to improve the church. The Hollidays and the Caldwells were instrumental among them. The front entrance of the church originally faced east toward Nelson Ferry Road, and was accessible by a long road leading up to the church. Taw Caw also had many great pastors who were instrumental in making innovative upgrades to the church property. Today Taw Caw Church remains in the same spot it has been for over one hundred years and the current pastor is Rev. William T. Johnson. From early on the membership and clergy had a vision and have never lost focus. The state-of-the-art Taw Caw Center adjacent to the church speaks to this effort.

At the age of 12, Willie Holliday Sr., was baptized at Taw Caw Baptist Church, outside in the church yard. It would be almost twenty years before a baptismal pool was built inside the church. Willie was probably baptized by Rev. E. W. Dix who served as pastor until 1911. In the Christian faith, Baptism is a religious rite and Holy Sacrament. Willie's baptism symbolized that he was now beginning a new life in Christ as a child of God and a part of the church family of believers. From day one, Willie Holliday Sr. was a faithful servant of the Lord. As an adult he became a church Deacon and all members loved and respected Deacon William Holliday Sr. Deacon Holliday was also the church sexton, performing maintenance, cleaning, filling the baptismal pool, and digging graves. He knew from memory where every deceased member was buried in the cemetery outside of the church.

According to Deacon John Evans Carter, "Deacon Holliday was responsible for ringing the church bell and was the only one who could do it. When a church member died the bell had to be rang three times in the morning. There was a technique to ringing the bell that only Deacon Holliday had perfected. When Deacon Holliday retired he turned the duty of ringing the bell over to me".

The church bell is very old-- really ancient. It is as old as the church if not older, with an estimated weight of 600 pounds. The bell sets high up in the church steeple and is only accessible by a set of small steps. Deacon Evans went on to explain that,

"Deacon Holliday said that enough force or pressure had to be put on the rope of the bell and it had to be pulled in such a way that it did not turn over. If it turned over it could tumble through the floor and that would be catastrophic". The bell also has a crack in it, making it equally dangerous. As a safety measure, it was decided shortly after Willie Holliday retired, not to ring the bell anymore, and the bell was also retired so to speak.

The bell had remained silent for many years but when Willie Holliday Sr. died in 2004, the bell was brought out of retirement and spruced up in order to be rang at his funeral. The ringing of the bell was an honor only fitting for a faithful church deacon. Today "Willie Holliday's Bell" sets silently in the church steeple.

The Reverend William T. Johnson,
Pastor of Taw Caw Missionary Baptist Church,
Remembers Deacon Willie Holliday Sr.

"The first time I saw Willie Holliday Sr., was around 1981, while I was applying to become a minister. He was always well-dressed. He walked with a long cane but it wasn't really a cane. It was shaped like a stick and it did not have the hook that canes have.

He kept a bottle of [green] alcohol in his pocket and would take out the bottle, put it up to his nose, and sniff. When he sniffed he would say "give me a moment, I get tangled up sometime". Other times he would say, "let me clear my head. This thing in my head is driving me crazy.

He did not believe in being late. He expected everyone to

be on time for meetings, etc.

Deacon Holliday knew the history of the church and everybody in it. He would tell you where to dig the graves in the Yard Section. He stopped ringing the church bell in 1982.

Deacon Holliday could always calm people down. He could talk to the angriest person and calm them down.

Once he stood with me and the other young deacons against the older deacons when they tried to overcome us. It took some courage for him to side with us younger deacons.

One thing about Deacon Holliday, he meant exactly what he said."

CHAPTER 4

TAW CAW SCHOOL TO SCOTT'S BRANCH SCHOOL

Scott's Branch Elementary School, Summerton,
South Carolina

Scott Branch School was originally named the Taw Caw School because it was started at Taw Caw Missionary Baptist Church during Reconstruction. Willie Holliday Sr.'s parents, April and Sarah Jane Holliday, and other black parishioners at the church raised money to start the school and keep it going. At that time the State of South Carolina did not provide schooling for black students so black churches donated land and labor to start schools for children. Clarendon County had sixty-one African-American schools like the Taw Caw School which were basically wooden structures that accommodated one or two classrooms. The students did not have desk but sat on wooden benches. Students were responsible for going in the fields to collect firewood to keep warm. Taw Caw's teachers were young women who had completed tenth grade but not Normal School. At that time teaching required two years of Normal school (teacher training) after high school as opposed to academics. The teachers at Taw Caw did not receive salaries but were paid in garden vegetables, eggs, chicken and other meats. Attendance was sporadic as students could not get to school when the weather was bad and picking cotton took priority over education. Black students in Clarendon County averaged a total of four years of education.

Willie Holliday started first grade at the Taw Caw School in the late 1800s. Willie's schooling was irregular because he was needed at home to pick cotton and help out on the farm. Nevertheless, Willie Holliday learned to read at a tenth grade level by reading the Holy Bible. According to grandson, Jim McKnight, "Grandpa read the bible which built up his reading skills".[7]

In the early 1900s Taw Caw's parents decided to move the school to Summerton. Once again April and Sarah Jane stepped to the plate along with other parents to raise the necessary funds. They settled on purchasing a lot beside the St. Mark A.M.E. Church.

The African-Methodist-Episcopal (A.M.E) denomination was founded by Richard Allen in Philadelphia in 1787, has been a pillar in black communities throughout

[9] Jim McKnight, *"It Was a Different Time for 109-year-old Clarendon Man,"* Times Extra, July 13, 2004, 3

the country. Richard Allen, born in slavery, started the church after experiencing numerous incidents of racism and injustice at the white St. George's Episcopal church in Philadelphia. Today Bishop Allen's original church, Mother Bethel, still exist. During slavery Mother Bethel was a major safe haven on the Underground Railroad. Runaway slaves were told to "look for Bethel" as they could always find lodging and safety at any A.M.E church. Summerton's St. Mark's A.M.E. was started by members of Liberty A.M.E.in 1885 who thought Liberty was too far to travel to.

After purchasing the lot by St. Mark A.M.E., the Taw Caw church members next purchased an old cotton gin house which they rolled it onto this site and made it into a classroom. A little brook named Scott's Branch ran behind the gin school and the church. It was little more than a "babbling brook", narrow and shallow, with an assortment of pebbles and rocks. But its name was beautiful and sounded serene, so Taw Caw parents decided to change the new school's name from Taw Caw to Scott's Branch.[8] Perhaps the parents identified also with the little brook as they, too, were forging a small, rocky path, in this case, into academia. Today the tiny brook named Scott's Branch that ran behind the gin school and the church is all dried up and just a narrow separation in the grass with pebbles and rocks scattered here and there. But the school that bears its name has survived.

The new school in the former gin house had two rooms. There was a wood burning stove to keep warm and the toilets were outside. When the school and St. Mark's church caught fire and burned down, parents once again pooled their meager resources to built another school. This second Scott's Branch

[10] Sbhaa, "Scott's Branch High School,",
http://www.scottsbranchhighalumni.com/aboutus.html. 2012

auditorium was converted into classrooms. In the meantime, St. Mark had been rebuilt, so the church was again used for school activities.[9]

In the Spring of 1937, another fire destroyed the school building. This time the parents decided to purchase the site on which the present Scott's Branch School stands at 1154 4th Street. The white frame building was built by the county, but the parents and teachers had to raise funds to put in electricity and water. For chapel, the students were marched from the white frame building to St. Mark. Commencement exercises were alternated between Taw Caw Baptist Church and Liberty Hill A.M.E churches. School plays were presented at Taw Caw. Jim McKnight remembers performing in a play held in St. Mark's auditorium since Scott's Branch School did not have one. This practice continued until the Gymtorium was constructed.[10]

Willie Holliday's daughter-in-law, Odessa McFadden Holliday, the wife of Willie's son, James, remembers, *"During the time I lived with an aunt, I attended a one-room school named Zoe Hill on highway 301 by J. Wesley Carter Road, in Summerton. Two of the teachers' names I remember are Louise Pearson and Amy Boatwright"*. Zoe Hill was a one-room school that came out of the reconstruction area. Mrs. McFadden-Holliday also attended Scott's Branch School and remembers "it was a long wood-frame building. There were no more than four or five teachers. There was an instructor named Anderson who "whipped with a paddle".

---

[9] Ibid.
[10] Ibid.

Mrs. Odessa Holliday, Daughter-in- Law

Wife of son James

Remembers Willie Holliday Sr

I was born January 29, 1931.

We used to go in the buggy to pick cotton. My Grandpa, Hampton Anderson, grew cotton and cucumbers. You had to plant something of your own to make money. He would take his cucumbers to Manning but if he couldn't get the price he wanted he would bring them right back and throw them away in the field.

Daddy had brought a piece of land and all of us worked clearing the trees. We got it looking real nice and the white man who sold it showed up and said he didn't sell it to daddy, he rented it. Daddy took the case to court but lost. It was a white man's word against his.

I remember the old Scott's Branch school. It was a long, wood frame building with 4 or 5 teachers. Anderson would whip us with paddles.

I went to Taw Caw Church with Mary Jane. He husband had the store.

My brother Anderson drove the school bus that the black parents brought to take their children to school (the bus that led to Briggs vs. Board). I went to Scott's Branch school but when I went to live with Aunt Leola I went to Zoe Hill School, a one-room school house off 301 by Wesley Carter Road.

I got married to James Holliday at 17 and we moved into Willie and Maggie Holliday's house. Mr. Willie was not much of a talker. He would eat and go to bed. Stella, Emma, Sank, and Pet were still home. Later James and I moved to Philadelphia. James used to drive the family car. It was a Ford. When we moved to Philadelphia, Stella wrote us a letter and saying, "send James back down here to drive the car".

When Grandpa (Willie Holliday Sr.) came to visit us in Philly, he slept right there on the couch.

Descendants Honor Willie Holliday Sr. with Academic Achievements

"If something comes to life in others because of you, then you have made an approach to immortality."

-- Norman Cousins

Willie Holliday Sr. was a farmer, a sower of the seed, and like any skilled farmer he understood you can't plant and reap in the same season. He sacrificed his own ambitions and aspirations in order to forge a path for his descendants. He was content to till the soil, plant the seeds, and take care of the fields and, consequently, he has reaped an abundant crop.

Willie Holliday Sr.'s descendants include entrepreneurs and many college graduates in a variety of professions-- medical doctors, marketing, business, military veterans, entrepreneurs, and government.

From the little Taw Caw School of 1886 to the best universities in the U.S., descendants of Willie Holliday Sr. honor him by sharing their academic successes.

Grandson Jim Mc Knight, "Boy Holliday", was the first college graduate in the family. He graduated from St. Peter's College in Jersey City, New Jersey, with two Bachelor's degrees; one in Business Administration and one in Business and Urban Community Development. (Jim, left, Standing with daughter Jenn McKnight)

Great-Granddaughter Serenity Holliday

Great-Great-Grandson Alex Payne

Great-Great-Granddaughter Leasia McKnight-Berklee
School of Music

-

\

GREAT-GRANDDAUGHTER JENNIFER MC KNIGHT IN MUSIC CLASS

JENN MCKNIGHT – CHAPEL HILL

ADDITIONAL GRADUATES IN ACCOMPLISHMENTS
SECTION

CHAPTER 5

DREAMS DIE YOUNG

According to an 1859 financial report, the South had three and half million slaves worth an aggregate value of sixteen hundred million dollars. It had 80,000 cotton plantations worth 125,000; 15,000 tobacco plantations worth 14 million; 206,000 sugar plantations worth 12 million; and 551 rice plantations worth 4 million.[11] In January 1865, Congress passed the Thirteenth Amendment abolishing slavery forever in America.

At the end of the Civil War the Georgetown-Charleston-Beauford area of South Carolina saw an influx of recently freed slaves while other counties had very few. Consequently, Black Codes were passed by southern whites forcing African-Americans to relocate out of the Charleston area to other areas. One of those forced to vacate was a black woman named Carolina Pearson-Johnson, who relocated to Clarendon County. She was chased out of Charleston with her two siblings who she never saw her again.

However, Clarendon County was looking promising for freed people. The Fifteenth Amendment of the Constitution gave citizens of every "race, color, or previous condition of servitude" the right to vote.

[11] New Orleans Delta. "Negroes and Cotton". Southern Cultivator, 1859, p. 282

A black minister and farmer from Clarendon county, J.D. Warley, was elected to the House of Representative and represented Clarendon County as a Congressman from 1870-1874 and as a Senator from 1874-1877. He was also active in the Republican party serving as election commissioner, magistrate, trial justice, and chairman of the Clarendon County Republican.

Mrs. Pearson-Johnson was another success story. After relocating to Clarendon County, she took the bull by the horns and became a successful entrepreneur acquiring a plantation with over 354 ½ acres of land. She supervised 32 farm families, sharecroppers and tenant farmers. In the 1890s she established the Johnson Mercantile Company on her plantation, one of the first cotton gins in Clarendon. Overall, blacks in Clarendon County, South Carolina, owned more land than those in any other county.

If the federal government had lived up to its Reconstruction promises, the lives of formerly freed blacks would have continued to improve. However, after over twenty years of trying to change the racist southern mindset, the federal government gave up and bailed out, leaving the freed people at the mercy of their former oppressors. With the feds out of the way, and no other opposition, in the 1890s embittered whites passed laws to disenfranchise African Americans which ended their participation in southern politics. The lives of blacks in Clarendon County and other southern states quickly went downhill afterwards. Education continued to be limited or nonexistent. Oppression in other areas also grew exponentially worse too and by the 1950s Summerton parents were forced to initiate a lawsuit against the school superintendent for bus transportation for their children, Briggs v Board. Seven of the original petitioners were relatives of Willie Holliday Sr.

The lawsuit was later combined with Brown vs. Board resulting in the 1954 landmark Supreme Court's decision to end school segregation.[12] (see photo of Jim McKnight in Epilogue reviewing the 21 petitioners cornerstone which was organized by him and installed by Prince Hall Masons at the First Stripped Bass Festival in the county).

The South is known for it beauty, peace, and tranquility but for young African-Americans like Willie Holliday that beauty, peace, and tranquility was marred by the ugliness of oppression. Challenging the law could bring swift and severe consequences. Willie's mother told him stories of the old days when she witnessed African American workers being beaten while working on the roads for not being productive.[13]

Willie probably mulled over the idea of going North but in the end he stayed because of his strong love for his family. Besides, he was a country boy at heart and always would be.

---

[12] Richard Kluger, Simple Justice: The History of Brown V. Board of Education and Black America's Struggle for Equality (New York, NY: Knopf Doubleday Publishing Group, 2011

Willie Holliday was born in what American History refers to as the "Gilded Age". The Gilded Age was era between the Civil

[13] Ibid.

War right up to the Progressive Era. In the words of Author Mark Twain, "an era of serious social problems masked by a thin gold gilding".

In the Gilded age, business tycoons rose up like weeds. John Pierpont Morgan was to investment banking, as what John D. Rockefeller was to oil, and as Andrew Carnegie to steel. In 1875, Steel tycoon Andrew Carnegie used money borrowed from J.P. Morgan's father's bank to construct the nation's largest steel plant in Pittsburgh, Pennsylvania. One hand washes the other. By 1885, steel skyscrapers appeared on Chicago's skyline and steel locomotives made up the first transcontinental rail line connecting California to Omaha, Nebraska. Between 1865 and 1890, railroads grew from 35,000 miles of track to 167,000 miles.[14] American cities were taken on industrial identities like New York City became known for clothing and fashion, and Chicago for meatpacking.

Since the 1860's, many Whites and African- Americans headed west seeking greener pastures in the Midwestern towns and the fertile valleys of California and Oregon.

[14] C. Berkin, C. Miller, R. Cherny, J. Gormly. *Making America: A History of the United States,* Wadsworth Cengage Learning, 2013, *Volume 2, 6th Ed., 454*

The Homestead Act of 1862 provided that any person could receive free as much as 160 acres of government land by building a house, living on the land for five years and farming on it. In the South, farming was also changing. Modern equipment like the gasoline tractor eliminated farm horse jobs. Many southerners migrated North where they worked and lived alongside European immigrants. By the 1920s when the Gilded Age met the Progressive Era, social and political reform groups rose up to counter all the social ills caused by the Gilded Age.

But the booming cities of the Gilded Age were located mostly in New England, the Middle Atlantic states, and the east North Central States.[15] Life for the Holliday family and other African-Americans in the South wasn't paved with gold and far less advanced.

The year of Willie Holliday's birth, 1893, the Civil War had been won almost thirty years ago, but the South was still sharply divided along racial lines and weighed down by legacy of slavery. Instead of moving on from the Civil War defeat, White southerners were still lamenting over the 'old south" which they romanticized as a place of "kindly plantation owners and loyal slaves". Further, they did not view themselves as losers of the Civil War but esteemed the Confederacy as heroes for risking life and limb to preserve good ole southern values.[16] Thus, throughout the South the Confederate flag and statues of Confederate soldiers were as common as apple pie.

In 1910, about 90 percent of all African Americans lived in the South. This would change by 1920 when as many as a half-million had moved north in what has been called the "Great Migration". Several factors contributed to

[15] Ibid., 503

[16] Ibid., 504

the migration but the most important were the brutality and hardship of southern life and the economic opportunities in the cities in the north.

Factories in the north needed workers and in the North you could earn as much in a day as in a week in the South. [17]

But life in the North also had a negative side. One of America's worst race riots sweep through the industrial city of East St. Louis, Illinois, on July 2, 1917, where thousands of black laborers from the south had relocated. Thirty-nine African Americans were killed in the riot and six thousand lost their homes.

On the 1910 census, 16-year-old Willie Holliday listed his occupation as "carpenter". Willie had learned carpentry from his grandfather, Stephen Caldwell, and was doing carpenter jobs and earning money. This was a strong indication that Willie desired to be something more than a sharecropper. Carpentry was also a safe alternative for a black male in a culture where "uppity" blacks were considered a threat. Willie understood that carpentry was a safe alternative that did not threatened the status quo. Sadly, in South Carolina in 1910, there weren't many job opportunities for black males outside of farming whether sharecropping, tenant farming, or working as farm hands.

[17] Ibid., 627

The sharecropping system provided a house and farmland even if it kept you perpetually in debt. Despite Willie's love for carpentry, it was just a matter of time before he followed in the footsteps of his dad and the other black males in Davis Station and embraced the plantation system of sharecropping.

CHAPTER 6

SHARECROPPING

WHAT'S MINE IS MINE AND WHAT YOURS
IS MINE TOO

The institution of sharecropping is often compared to slavery, however, sharecropping was more of an economic injustice than a racial one. Black landowners also leased land out to poor farmers and poor white farmers were also sharecroppers or half-croppers. As history points out, only a small percentage of white southerners were wealthy plantation owners, the rest were left jobless too when Union soldiers destroyed big plantations. The Freedman's Bureau was established to help poor whites as well as blacks get reestablished.

Sharecropping as practiced after the Civil War was the result of President Johnson returning the land confiscated during the Civil War back to the former slave owners. In January 1865, General William T. Sherman issued Special Field Order No. 15, setting aside the Sea Islands and land along the South Carolina coast for freed families. By June of that year, forty thousand freed people had settled on 400,000 acres of "Sherman Land".[18] This resulted in a rallying cry that freed slaves would be awarded "forty acres and a mule".[19]

General Oliver O. Howard, head of the Freedman's Bureau, controlled 850,000 acres of land abandoned by former slave owners or confiscated from Confederate Leaders.[20] General Howard was ready to move forward with 40-acre plots to freed people when President Andrew Johnson ordered him to halt land redistribution. What worse, Johnson ordered him to reclaim land already given out to freed people. African Americans who had

[18] Ibid. 426

[19] ibid
[20] Ibid

already taken over their 40 acres felt betrayed. Many had fought with Sherman for what they considered "a heap of freedom they didn't git".[21]

Consequently, the former plantation owners had all the land and poor whites and freed African-Americans had none. The former plantation class could not hire workers to farm the land because southern money was worthless.

The Freedman's Bureau assisted in helping freed blacks and poor whites rent land from wealthy landowners. The head of the family signed a contract with the landowner to rent a plot of land. The contract might include renting supplies such as a mule, farm tools, seed, and fertilizer from the same landowner or another creditor. These contracts were called crop liens, similar to a mortgage, based on the use of crops as collateral for extension of credit by a merchant.[22] Once signed the merchant had a lien (legal claim) on the growing crop.[23]

Many merchants ran stores and included in the contract was often a clause requiring the renter to patronize the merchant's store and no other. It goes without saying that more often than not, the rent and debt owed to the landowner exceeded the value of the entire harvest. What worse, the crop lien was automatically renewed if all debts were not paid by end of a year.[24] In addition to the economic power the landowner held over the renter, the landlord often exercised political power by requiring sharecroppers to vote for the candidates they supported. Failure to comply could result in eviction from the land and loss of credit.

[22] Ibid., 427
[23] Ibid.
[24] Ibid.

It was a system equivalent to leading a lamb to slaughter but what other options did poor people have? For African-Americans, the only difference between slavery and sharecropping was that they had slightly more control over their daily lives but they were no better off economically.

In other words, Sharecropping was a system of "what's mine is mine and what's yours is mine too"

One of the black landowners who leased land to sharecroppers was Carolina Pearson-Johnson. She was born in Georgetown, South Carolina in the 1820s but was forced out of the area at the end of the Civil War because too many former slaves were living in the Georgetown-Charleston-Beauford, South Carolina areas and not enough in the midlands and Piedmont areas. Mrs. Johnson relocated to Clarendon County where she met and married Isaac Johnson. The couple had two children, William and Annie. Mrs. Johnson went on to become a successful entrepreneur and acquired a plantation with over 354 ½ acres of land.

She supervised 32 farm families, some sharecroppers, some tenant farmers. In the 1890s she established the Johnson Mercantile Company on her plantation, one of the first cotton gins in Clarendon. Interestingly, Ms. Johnson was not educated and signed her name with an X but her success is a legacy to young people. Mrs. Johnson died on September 27, 1931. A cemetery named in the honor of Carolina Johnson is located in Manning near the Wyboo Plantation.[25]

---

[25] Emily Vaughn. *Carolina Pearson-Johnson*. Blacks Establish Town of Summerton. emilyevaughn.com. 2008

Tenant farming was another option for former slaves. Tenant farmers were more independent than sharecroppers. They didn't own the land they farmed either but they were completely in charge of their crops from start to finish. They were responsible for all the necessary supplies and got to select the crops they wanted to raise. The entire harvest was theirs to sell or use as needed. They paid landowners rent in cash or a share of the crop. It was a challenge but many manage to save money and buy their own land. parcels of land.[26]

Sharecropping and tenant farming began to fade in the 1930s when Congress passed laws to help farmers acquire their own land. Congress also worked to improve conditions for sharecroppers and tenant farmers. The mechanization of agriculture and the growth of urban employment furthered the decline of sharecroppers and tenant farmers in the twentieth century.[27]

[26] Benson, Sonia, et al. "Sharecropping and Tenant Farming." UXL Encyclopedia of U.S. History, vol. 7, UXL, 2009, pp. 1400-1401.

CHAPTER 7

WILLIE & MAGGIE

WILLIE & MAGGIE HOLLIDAY

On December 6, 1916, Willie Holliday and Maggie McFadden got married. According to the marriage certificate, Willie was 23 and Maggie was 18 ½. Actually Maggie was 17 and would turn 18 the following May. The couple traveled by borrowed wagon to the Probate Court in Manning, South Carolina, over the old Tobacco Roads that existed since slavery times when wagons carrying tobacco cut paths through the countryside on their way to market. It wouldn't be until the 1940s that these dirt roads and forged paths in the densely wooded pine forest would become U.S. 301.[28] Willie and Maggie were united in matrimony by J.M. Windham, Judge of Probate. It was a simple affair. The couple said their "I do's" and were on their way. The trip to Manning and back took up the whole day.

South Carolina had no law requiring marriage licenses until 1911. Until then, marriages were legal if performed by ministers and common law marriages were also recognized.

Slaves were not permitted to marry as marriage laws would have given couples rights over each other that conflicted with slave owners' rights. Although enslaves couples may have participated in a "jumping the broomstick" ceremony to show they were in a committed relationship, jumping the broom is not unique to black culture. It originated in 18th century Britain and means "sham marriage".

Willie had met Maggie at Taw Caw Baptist Church where

they both were members. Maggie's parents, Davis and Adrianna McFadden were life long members of Taw Caw. Maggie's father was born in 1862 and raised by his mother Emma Mc Fadden. He had a younger sister, Sissy. In adulthood Davis adopted the first name Jeff and was known by all as Jeff Davis or J.D. His death certificate lists his father as Niagra McFadden.

Maggie's mother Adrianna was born in 1864 to Primus and St. Francis (Henrietta) Butler. Both of Maggie's parents grew up in Davis Station. Jeff Davis McFadden and Adrianna Butler were married in 1884. The couple had ten children. Maggie was born on May 15, 1899 and was next to the youngest child. She had a younger brother. Maggie indicated on the 1940 Census that she attended school up to fifth grade.

Sadly, Maggie's mother Adrianna passed away on March 10, 1915, at age 52. Maggie was fifteen at the time and it was undoubtedly painful for her to lose her mother at the age where she is growing into womanhood. After Adrianna's death, Jeff Davis married a younger woman named Rachel and soon had two daughters, Viola and Elma.

Perhaps it was the loneliness of losing her mom to an early death and competing with another woman for her father's attention that propelled Maggie into a relationship with Willie Holliday Sr. At 23, Willie was a bachelor but once the young, beautiful Maggie caught his eye he was captivated. It is unknown how long the two were courting but a year after her mother's death Maggie married Willie. Maggie could have stepped right out of Proverbs 31, "a virtuous wife more precious than rubies". She was indeed the good and supportive wife Willie needed and a nurturing mother. People remember Maggie as quiet, calm and self-confidant. The life and legacy of Willie Holliday Sr., cannot be understood without taking into account Maggie who was the love of his life. Willie was a good man but Maggie helped him be a better man. She loved her children, corrected them when she needed to and imposed very high standards.

After Willie asked Jeff Davis McFadden for his daughter Maggie's hand in marriage, Willie set about putting down roots. Carpenter jobs were few and far between and didn't pay the bills, therefore, Willie went to see Mr. Plowden about leasing a plot of land to farm. Soon he would be a married man and had to support his bride and provide a home. It was the beginning of Willie's career as a sharecropper. Mr. Plowden was a big landowner in Summerton. Later Willie would sharecrop for Mr. Touchberry, another big landowner. For Willie, young, southern black man of limited means, sharecropping was undoubtedly the only real job available. The landowner provided the land, house, mule, seed, fertilizer, and farm equipment so as a sharecropper, Willie contracted half of all commercial grown crop as well as the labor of him and family back to the landowner. Other expenses included axel grease for the wagon (sometimes given by landowner), mule harness, fee for grinding the corn for grits and corn meal.

First on the agenda was building a house. The house Willie built tells the sad story of sharecropping. It wasn't the house he wanted for his bride and he promised he would make it up to her as soon as he could. But at the time materials were costly and had to be paid back out of crop earnings so Willie had to skimp. He went in hock for lumber, nails, and roofing material. The end result was a shanty-kind-of-house; wood frame whose inside walls were plank boards with little insulation. It had a tin roof with a wooden porch. The windows were wooden slats and had no glass but closed with shutters. The house set on brick stilts. It had a wood burning fireplace and drinking water came from a well. The house had three rooms and every inch of space was used for sleeping, sitting, cooking, and eating. Something on the ramshackle property was always in need of repair, whether it was a shingle on the roof or a loose nail falling off the door hinge. But Willie was thankful to have a roof over his head. If there was anything beautiful about the house it was the wild cherry trees growing in the yard. Beauty was in the simple things like hummingbirds and butterflies dancing around the Palmetto trees and the scent of Yellow Jessamines (called Jasmines in other parts of the country) permeating the air.

But Willie and Maggie were in love and being together was all that mattered. It wasn't Maggie's nature to complain anyway. She was low-key with a pleasant disposition. The couple's first child was born on October 16, 1917, a baby girl they named Bertha. A year later they had another baby girl named Maggie Lee after her mother and called Lee. Maggie spent her days raising the children, keeping house, and canning blackberries and peaches. She made great biscuits too. Maggie's trademark was the heavy weight quilts she sewed for those cold, southern nights. The quilts were described as "weighing a ton". They were so heavy that once you covered up you were pretty much stuck underneath.

Willie wasn't one to complain either. You never heard him lamenting over the obstacles of sharecropping. He was a person who was clear about his principles and morals. A man took care of his family, end of story.

The months of April through October was the growing season. It was a time that sharecroppers prayed for a plentiful harvest and worked their butts off to make it happen. But no matter how plentiful the crop or how great the work ethic, the crop was never plentiful enough for Willie and other sharecroppers to make a big profit or put a dent in their debt to the landowner. Were they being cheated? Possibly. Once the crop was turned over to the landowner it was out of their hands and a black man knew better to question a white man's integrity. The black sharecroppers held on to a small dose of hope that the landowner would do right by them.

Willie Holliday's mornings started with him getting out of bed first and building a fire to warm up the house. He never, ever, let Maggie get up until after he built a fire and the house was warm. Then in the evenings after a hard day in the fields, Willie ended his day with a nice dinner and retired to the rickety front porch where he sat with his feet propped on the wooden rail and could often be heard whistling. That is how he got one of his nicknames, "Bird".[29]

Sometimes Maggie joined him on the porch where they sat and talked until it got so dark you couldn't see your hand in front of you. "Boy" shared a touching detail. He remembers his grandparents sitting on the porch together as happy as the first day they married. The fact that they were happy despite living such a simple life with very little left a lasting impression on his young mind.

In April 2, 1917, a few months after Willie and Maggie got married, President Woodrow Wilson asked Congress to declare war on Germany. The other nations had been engaged in war since 1914, however, Woodrow Wilson had chosen to remain neutral. But that March when German U-boats sunk six American ships Wilson asked Congress to go to the war. On May 7, 1915, a The U.S. Army and National Guard was short of manpower so in May Congress passed the Selective Services Act requiring men ages 21 – 30 (later changed from 18- 45)   to register with local draft boards.

Nearly 400,000 African Americans served during World

War I. 200,000 served overseas, 30,000 on the front line and the rest doing menial tasks. African Americans served in segregated units, many in the Army, and the Navy limited African Americans to food service. The Marines did not allow African Americans to serve at all. 600 African Americans earned commissions as officers but only had authority over other black troops.[30] It wasn't until 1948 that President Truman signed a law to desegregate the armed forces.

Willie Holliday registered for the draft as required, however, he was given Sharecropper's protection. Sharecropping was big business and carried political clout.

"Sharecroppers protection" could also be used to get out of jail. Farm production of cotton and crops were essential to the war effort because America was also supplying its allies with food because European agriculture was severely disrupted. Americans were asked to conserve food through "Meatless Mondays" and "Wheat less Wednesdays" as well as by planting "war gardens" to raise vegetables. Therefore, Willie Holliday served his country as a farmer.

In today's modern world it is hard to imagine life without electric lights and indoor plumbing. Imagine if you can, no bathrooms so you have to use an outhouse or privy. There was no toilet paper either so you had to think of other options. Drinking water was fetched from a well or creek. Vegetables had to be planted by hand then picked from the garden. Meals were cooked over a wood-burning stove. The stove was also used to keep warm so firewood had to be gathered and cut. Hogs were slaughtered then the meat cured in order to preserve it because there was no refrigeration. Something called an ice box could hold a block of ice and keep things call for a short period of time. Clothes were washed in big pots over fire. You had to get buckets of water and gather firewood to make a fire to warm the water up. The same thing with taking baths which were done in a tin tub or washing your hair. Water always had to get toted and fire wood was needed to make the fire to warm up the water. And if you got sick there was a folk remedy to cure whatever ailed you because there was no money for doctors. Homework or reading was done by Kerosene lamp. There was no television and listening to radio required electricity-- which wasn't available. Kerosene Oil was expensive and you avoided "burning the midnight oil" whenever possible. At nightfall there was not much else to do but go to bed with the chickens so to speak. Life for the Hollidays was use-it-up, wear-it-out, make-it-do, and learn-to-do-without.

Willie and Maggie's life may have seen decimated on the surface but in actuality they were quite happy because they didn't make their life about 'things". Willie and Maggie would have ten children altogether, six daughters and four sons. The children were Bertha, Maggie, Willie, Jr., John, James, Stella, Emma, Edward, Leanese(Sank), and Dorothy (Pet).

Willie Holliday, Sr., took in a grandson called "Boy" from age 3 to 15 and raised him as his own. Boy was the son of Maggie Lee and husband, Blaney McKnight. Boy says he was "born in a little old stick house at J. W. Carter Road". J.W. Carter Road is significant because it was the school district line that was the basis for Briggs vs Elliott.

Boy was around of the same age as many of his aunts and uncles and they grew up together alternating between playing and fighting as most kids do. One of Boy's first memories is crying when his aunts and uncles teased him about not having a mother or father. The taunt went something like this, "poor little boy ain't got no mother, ain't got no father". Of course, Boy did have a mother who was the children's older sister, Maggie Lee. Boy's father Blaney often came looking for him and Boy remember hiding under the bed. Blaney would stoop down to tie his shoe and probably saw Boy under the bed but he knew better than to cross Willie Holliday Sr.

Sometimes the children's games got too rough like the time his Uncle Edward, called "Brother", shot Boy with a toy bow and arrow. Boy remembers crying himself to sleep on his grandmother's lap. Boy remembers that after the Japanese bombed Pearl Harbor they were petrified of being blown up so when the Dust Croppers flew overhead spraying powder over the corn fields, Boy and the other children would throw hub caps and other stuff up at the planes. They thought the dust croppers were Japanese war planes.

Boy would grow up as "Boy Holliday" and stay with his grandparents until aged 15 when he relocated to Jersey City, New Jersey to live with his mother. Boy was the first family member to serve in the military, serving four years in the United States Air Force. He was also the first college graduate in the family, graduating from St. Peter's College in Jersey City, N.J., with two Bachelor's degrees; one in Business Administration and one in

Business and Urban Community Development. Boy continued his efforts as a Business and Economic Development Consultant until retiring. Interestingly, Boy was also the first entrepreneur in the family. In mid-1960s he started M & M Beauty Supply Distributorship in Harlem and in 1974 he purchased Lester's Hair Products.

Amid the hardships of poverty, Willie Holliday, Sr. set examples for the children through word and deed. He had unbelievable resilient and perseverant. The houses he built are on forgotten roads covered in weeds and lost in time. The fertile fields where he farmed are barren.

A few trees the children used to climb are still there. President Roosevelt's "New Deal", President Kennedy's "New Frontier, nor President Johnson's "Great Society", did nothing to alleviate the family's abject poverty. Willie Holliday Sr. was the glue that held the family together. He planted something that could never to be sold or taken away and that was hope. The soil was rich in hope.

Rev. Dr. Willie Robinson (Grandson)

Pastor of Mt. Pleasant Baptist Church

Remembers his Grandfather Willie Holliday Sr.

I did my first sermon at Taw Caw.

Grandpa was a walking history. He knew where every grave was at Taw Caw without Tombstones. Grandpa didn't live his life by adages. He motivated people by the way he lived. He was big on work ethic and being on time. I remember one day when we went to church together we were an hour early. When he talked you wanted to write it down. I remember visiting and it being so dark you "have to pipe in sunlight". Grandma Maggie made these handmade quilts that were so heavy that once she laid it over you, you couldn't get up. She would suggest to use the bathroom before you laid down. Once my wife called her "Grandma Maggie" and she said don't call me grandma, call me Miss Maggie, it sounds younger." When Grandpa came to visit us in Baltimore, he would have my room and I would sleep in the basement.

The two land owners Grandpa worked for were the Plowdens and the Touchberrys.

CHAPTER 8

LIFE ON THE FARM

WILLIE HOLLIDAY WITH GREAT-
GRANDSONS JIM JR., MIKE, & GERRARD MC
KNIGHT

Farming was essentially "all hands on deck". According to
Boy, "Crops had to be planted by hand and everyone in the

household had a job to do, children included. No one was allowed to be lazy. Goals were set for cotton picking like 100 pounds by aged 8. Grandpa considered schooling secondary to the farm contract. You could attend school but you had to work too. If you failed school, then you had to work the fields chopping and picking cotton every day except Sunday. Then on Sunday you had to prepare for church and Sunday school. The preparation that went into preparing for church and traveling roundtrip by mule and wagon, did not leave much time for play, even on Sunday which was the only possible day we had to play. Point is, grandpa kept us all busy. His feeling was that too much idol time was not good. Believe me, the living up to farm contract, taking care of animals, mule, pigs, cows, chicken, garden, was a full-time job for all.

The farm contract was for cotton and corn. Farming was done the old fashioned way. Everything was planted by hand then had to be picked by hand. The sharecropping contract included the land, house, mule, wagon, seeds and fertilizer, all provided by the landowner. Everything else had to be paid for out of sharecropping profits—which weren't a lot to begin with-- or gotten from the company store against profits. These items included personal garden stuff, household items, rice, flour, salt, and pepper. In addition to working on the contract, we had to eat too. Meats were the major items and included chicken, hogs, duck, cow, fish. The hog was raised and prepared and stored for curing (smoked and hung in the barn until needed). Beef was Farming was essentially "all hands on deck". According to Boy, "Crops had to be planted by hand and everyone in the household had a job to do, children included. No one was allowed to be lazy. Goals were set for cotton picking like 100 pounds by aged 8. Grandpa considered schooling secondary to the farm contract. You could attend school but you had to work too. If you failed school, then you had to work the fields chopping and picking cotton every day except Sunday. Then on Sunday you had to prepare for church and Sunday school. The preparation that went into preparing for church and traveling roundtrip by mule and wagon, did not leave much time for play, even on Sunday which was the only possible day we had to play. Point is, grandpa kept us all busy. His feeling was that too much idol time was not good. Believe me, the living up to farm contract, taking care of animals, mule, pigs, cows, chicken, garden, was a full-time job for all.

The farm contract was for cotton and corn. Farming was done the old fashioned way. Everything was planted by hand then had to be picked by hand. The sharecropping contract included the land, house, mule, wagon, seeds and fertilizer, all provided by the landowner. Everything else had to be paid for out of sharecropping profits—which weren't a lot to begin with-- or gotten from the company store against profits. These items included personal garden stuff, household items, rice, flour, salt, and pepper. In addition to working on the contract, we had to eat too. Meats were the major items and included chicken, hogs, duck, cow, fish. The hog was raised and prepared and stored for curing (smoked and hung in the barn until needed). Beef was kept as long as it could. Ice was kept in the fireplace in the summer. The two-hour trip by mule and wagon was a real issue due to ice melting.

We raised chickens, a hog, a vegetable garden of our own and grandpa caught fish when he could. In the evenings we would go in the corn fields and pick up left over corn that had dropped. We didn't think of it as stealing because the corn had dropped. We would pick it up and have it ground into meal.

Stella Holliday Robinson was quoted in the article "Toiling & Thanking God", as saying "Soon as it begins daylight, you had to get up. He (daddy) be calling you. If it was cotton you had to hoe by hand, or if it was time you would pick".

In the same article, John Holliday (Willie's son) is quoted as saying, "You had to obey him. You didn't talk back. And nobody was allowed to be lazy. Labor began at ages 5 or 6 and expectations were high. When I was 5, I picked 50 pounds. When

I was 8, I picked 100.

When I was 11, I picked 200. Everyone had chores. Do the chickens. Dig potatoes. Get firewood. Pick cotton. Pull corn. When work for others was done, work waited at home".[31]

The Great Depression brought hardship to farmers as well as everyone else. In 1933, Congress passed the The Agricultural Adjustment Act (AAA) in which the government paid farmers for not producing a lot of crop. The government believe that surpluses drove prices down cutting production was a way to make a profit and get paid extra by the government.

The plan proved successful but unfortunately sharecroppers and tenant farmers could not participate in the

[31] Ibid.

program nor did they receive a share of the money. In fact, it backfired on them because less production meant less crops needed and by the end of 1935, a million sharecroppers had been evicted because the government was paying landowners to take their land out of production.[32]

Food

Grits and Cornmeal were two major food items. Both are made from corn. After the corn was harvested, what was left after harvest, was picked up and taken to the mill to have ground into meal and grits.

---

[32] C. Berkin, C. Miller, R. Cherny, J. Gormly. *Making America: A History of the United States,* Wadsworth Cengage Learning, 2013, *Volume 2, 6th Ed., 703*

In the south, grits are a symbol of its diet, its customs, its humor, and its hospitality.[33] The word "grits" derives from the Old English word "grytt," meaning coarse meal. Grits are a food made from corn that is ground into a coarse meal and then boiled. Hominy grits are a type of grits made from hominy with the germ removed, which is corn that has been treated with an alkali in a process called nixtamalization. Grits are of American origin and are similar to other thick maize-based porridges from around the world such as polenta and mieliepap.

Traditionally, the hominy for Grits was ground on a stone mill. The ground hominy is then passed through screens, the finer sifted material used as grit meal, and the coarser as Grits. Many American communities used a gristmill until the mid-twentieth century, farmers bringing their corn to be ground, and the miller keeping a portion as his fee.

Cornmeal is a meal ground from dried corn. It is a common staple food, and is ground to fine, medium, and coarse consistencies, but not as fine as wheat flour.

According to Boy, "Grandpa would go in debt for grits and cornmeal because depending on the success of the crop, grits and cornmeal may be all we had to eat. Grits could be paired with anything –sausage, ham, tomatoes-- and corn meal could be made into mush. My family ate three meals a day --breakfast, dinner, and supper—sun-up, noon, and sun-down. The breakfast menu extended from cornbread & milk to fatback (pork bacon) and grits. Corn was also used to feed the pigs".

"Our dinners included cabbage and cornbread, cured ham, fish, chicken & rice. My family's daily meals came mostly from the woods and garden (peas, mitten corn, cabbage, okra, white potatoes and sweet potatoes. Food was stored in the ground and barn in the winter, and in the Spring and Summer we fished and grew a garden".

SWEET POTATOE BANK

The sweet potato had been a staple food for black people since slavery. Sweet Potatoes are eaten various ways such as Sweet Potato Pie, candied sweets, sweet potato pudding, and baked sweet potatoes.

Sweet potatoes could be kept throughout the year in potatoes banks. Potato banks were a method of storing potatoes by burying them in the ground covered with pine straw and dirt as sweet potatoes were a year around necessity. According to Boy, "We were not allowed to pick sweet potatoes before season (the first frost) but sometimes a hard rain would flood the fields and our feet would sink down into the mud and allow an early picking and to us kids that was a premium. We would roast them in the fire place chimney in the living room by burying them under hot hickory or oak wood ashes. After the ashes cooked them we would peel off the skin. It was our only snack. We got candy only at Christmas.

The sweet potato (Ipomoea batatas) is a dicotyledonous plant that belongs to the bindweed or morning glory family, Convolvulaceae. Its large, starchy, sweet-tasting, tuberous roots are a root vegetable. The young leaves and shoots are sometimes eaten as greens. The plant is an herbaceous perennial vine, bearing alternate heart-shaped or palmately lobed leaves and medium-sized sympetalous flowers. The edible tuberous root is long and tapered, with a smooth skin whose color ranges between yellow, orange, red, brown, purple, and beige. Its flesh ranges from beige through white, red, pink, violet, yellow, orange, and purple. Sweet potato cultivars with white or pale yellow flesh are less sweet and moist than those with red, pink or orange flesh.

The soft, orange sweet potato is often called a "yam" in parts of North America, the sweet potato is botanically very distinct from a genuine yam (Dioscorea), which is native to Africa and Asia and belongs to the monocot family Dioscoreaceae.

COME BUTTER SONG

Grandma Maggie would shake the cream from the milk in a chilled glass jar while singing a song she made up *"come butter come, come butter come, the fish is in the water now come butter come"*. She would sing sometimes for hours until the butter became butter.

Shaking the cream is similar to Churning, a process of shaking up cream (or whole milk) to make butter, and various forms of butter. Milk and butter came from the cow and goat. Butter making was done by hand and in butter churns. Butter is essentially the fat of milk and is usually made from sweet cream.

CHAPTER 9

BOY'S LIFE WITH GRANDPA-IN HIS OWN WORDS

Willie Holliday Sr. with Grandson Jim McKnight "Boy" & Great-Granddaughter Jenn

Fish was an excellent source of food but Willie had little time to fish and hardly any money to buy fish. After I became skillful at fishing by being a fishing guide for the Wilcox's and their guest, I was able to supplement the families meager fare. I also provided food from another source. Children were expected to work on the farm by ages 5 or 6. They were given age-appropriate chores and reasonable production quotas. Unfortunately, I could not get the hang of farm work. I gave it my best shot but I was just hopeless at everything. Of course this drew the wrath of grandpa.

JIM MC KNIGHT RETURNS TO THE WILCOX
FAMILY HOME IN SUMMERTON IN 2017

I decided it was better to disappear than stand around doing nothing or doing everything wrong. about a mile up the road from our house I met two playmates, Harold and Freddie Wilcox, who were younger than me. the Wilcox family was White and I was soon spending everyday playing with newfound friends and eventually their dad hired him to look after the two boys and cut the lawn at a fee. at aged 12, Mr. Wilcox gave me the keys to the car, taught me to drive the car so I could drive the boys to school.

in a twist of fate, the Wilcox family had a black cook who would often shared leftovers with me which i took home to the family. sometimes these leftovers were all the family had to eat. i gained newfound respect in grandpa's eyes for my resourcefulness. The maid also taught me how to keep out of trouble with white folks.

I remember an incident that occurred where I drew Grandpa's wrath. Grandpa sent me out for George Washington smoking tobacco. There was a Christmas parade going on and after the parade the children got candy. I made a decision to hang around until after the parade was over. When I returned home 2 hours later Grandpa was fit to be tied. I never remember him so angry. He took a branch from the tree and whipped me until grandma stopped him. The whipping caused me to revisit the importance of being on time and a lesson in prioritizing your mission. My mission is not allowing anything to be a victim of falling through the cracks of history.

Uncle John left and move to Philly, but before leaving he worked at CCC Camp building the Santee River Dam. His family concern always stood out to me as he would bring from his CCC job left-over Rice Krispies to share with the family and boy was that a treat for all of us. He maintained his family concern after moving to Philly by bringing back candy bars (Oh Henrys) for each member of the family. Us kids looked forward to his visits once a year and the candy bars. We loved him for the candy bars. This was remembered by me when Uncle John had an interest in starting his own business after leaving the ship yard and I gave him my support.

GRANDPA'S FOLK MEDICINE REMEDIES

Grandpa still surprises me in his abilities to survive. I always knew him to be a strong man. He practiced folk medicine and survived on home made remedies. This was due to mainly to the shortage of doctors, racist standards in the treatment of African-Americans, as well as his medical upbringing which led him to rely on home remedies until the age of 80 when he had his first doctor's visit.

Grandpa's home made remedies ranged from home made salve for hemorrhoids, sassafras tea for colds, and hot cow manure for cuts. We would step in the manure and stand in it a minute or two. It worked to help the healing process. He used Devil's shoe string (a vine root) for back aches, and a spider web and kerosene mix for cuts. Other roots included sheep droppings and sugar/syrup for whooping cough, and grass root tea for fever. Some other roots were Joseph Coats, Mullett leaves, gum tree berries, and many others. Whatever the pain, grandpa found the medicine. Grandpa's friends could testify to his skills and methods. They often went to him for advice and help and believed in his ability to cure.

Grandpa's efforts to survive and stay well inspired me to accept a contract with the town of Summerton to establish a medical center in 1979, the Summerton Medical Clinic. I was reminded of grandpa's home made remedies to survive and my paternal grandmother, Grandma Charlotte, and long wait in doctor's lines which ranged from hours to the next day. Previously, Summerton residents had to travel to Manning and often had to wait for a once-a-week bus ride to the doctor. I traveled from New Jersey to Summerton to assist in the development of the Summerton Medical Clinic. It was a proud thing in light of my childhood memories of limited medical services.

KEEPING TRADITION ALIVE

It is understandable for African Americans to reject farming, associating it with slavery and four hundred years of forced labor in the tobacco, cotton, and rice fields of the South. But It is important to know that Africans were farmers before they were slaves and farming is an important part of our African heritage that should be embraced.

History shows that Africans brought extensive agrarian or agriculture knowledge to America. They were highly skilled when it came to growing tobacco, cotton, and rice. More importantly, rice. White farmers were unable to grow rice successfully but once it was revealed that West Africans was highly skilled rice growers, West Africans became a high commodity in the Atlantic Slave Trade. In addition to West Africans' extensive knowledge in rice cultivation, Africans were also more adaptable to Carolina's climate and landscape which resembled their homeland of Africa.

But what was advantageous to the white plantation owners was not advantageous to Africans who found themselves in captivity on America's rice plantations. The rice plantations were the worst place Africans could end up. The rice fields were moist and wrought with diseases. Reptiles lurked in low waters. But, sadly, despite the adverse working conditions, Africans did not have options. It was work or be punished or killed.

Today we must recognize African agricultural knowledge as a valuable asset that single-handedly built America's agricultural economy. Whether it was tobacco, cotton, or rice, Africans were natural agrarians. Let us honor our African ancestor's knowledge and not allow it to be tarnished by the negativity of slavery.

WILLIE HOLLIDAY SR.'S GREAT-GRANDS EMBRACING AFRICAN AGRARIAN HERITAGE & GIVING HONOR TO THEIR GREAT-GRANDFATHER

Great-Great Grandsons Alex
& Kaz picking apples

Great-Great Grandson Alex
planting garden

Aurora picking Kale from Brother Alex' Garden

Great-Great-Grandson Alex grows a

watermelon

Great-Great Granddaughter Aurora
busy in garden

KAZ & AURORA WORKING IN GARDEN

CHAPTER 10

FAMILY STORIES

Every family have stories. The following stories recall happy moments, disappointments, most cherished thoughts, extreme adversities, and everything in between.

The Preacher Story

Boy lived in Grandpa's house from ages four to sixteen years old remembers how the children abhorred the preacher's visits. He and the other children, his young aunts and uncles, had a problem with the preacher visiting because for one thing it meant chicken was going to be served and the preacher was going to eat up all the chicken. Meat was precious. It wasn't served on a regular basis and when it was they didn't need the preacher there eating it up.

However, there was a certain level of excitement attached to the preacher's visit, mainly because the preacher drove a car and cars excited the children They would walk around repeating "Ca' is coming here". The excitement grew the longer the day got until finally they saw the car in the distance as it made its way down dusky road 301. The preacher had arrived to eat up all the chicken.

The Cow Story

One of the saddest stories is the Cow story. A family emergency arose that required the cow being sold for money. The children cried and moped around for a couple of days. Not that they were affectionately attached to the cow like one is to a pet. They understood that farm animals were not pets and are raised to be eaten. The children were sad because there would be no more milk to go with the cornmeal mush.

Grandpa and the Deer

One-day Willie Holliday Sr. entered the barn and encountered a buck (deer) inside eating the corn. Willie grabbed a hammer and took the deer on. A fight ensued between Willie and the deer. The deer was trying to hook Willie in the groan and Willie beating it off with a hammer while hollering for help. Fortunately, family members heard the call for help and ran to the barn. They managed to chase the deer. Willie wasn't hurt and the deer went on about his business.

Buster Argues with Sheriff

Buster (Willie Holliday Jr.) went to town one night and got into an argument with the sheriff. He ran two miles back to the house to get a gun to go back and shoot the sheriff. The family had to everything they could to hold Buster to keep him from going back out the door. Grandpa grabbed the gun and was trying to wrestle the gun from Buster. Grandpa was tussling with him and Boy grabbed hold of Buster's leg. I locked onto his leg and just hung on to it. We were in a stale mate. Buster finally calmed down. Grandpa discourage him from going back by preventing him from doing it.

Kill You or Cure you

Grandma Maggie was having trouble swallowing and Grandpa went and got this   gray stuff in a whiskey bottle. It was roots but it worked. She took some and something came up and then she could breathe again. I have seen roots work. The stuff will either kill you or cure you.

CHAPTER 11

BROTHERLY LOVE LODGE #99 – PRINCE HALL
AFFLIATES

SEE **OLDEST MAN,** PAGE 11A

In 1952, Willie Holliday, Sr., is believed to have help found Brotherly Love Lodge No. 99, Prince Hall Affiliated, Free Masons in Manning, S.C. Willie Holliday, Sr., served as the Worshipful Master and Past Master. The office of Worshipful Master is the highest honor to which a lodge may appoint any of its members.

In addition to Willie Holliday, Sr., other known family members who are Prince Hall masons:

- Jim McKnight'
- Blaney McKnight
- Michael McKnight
- Gerard McKnight
- Melvin McKnight
- Willie Holliday, Jr.

The Order of the Eastern Star was established in Boston in 1850 as an auxiliary organization of wives, mothers, daughters, and sisters of Freemasons. It became affiliated with the Prince Hall Masons in 1874 through the founding of the Queen Esther

Chapter No. 1 in Washington, D.C. The Eastern Star conducts its own philanthropic and community service activities as well as supporting the work of the male lodges.

The Holliday family have two members who were Eastern Stars:

- Maggie Mc Fadden Holliday

Sallie Holliday (spouse of Willie Holliday Jr.) Past Matron of Queen Esther, Chapter No. 2, Prince Hall Affiliation, Jersey City, NJ

-

-

Oct 31, 2017

(Brotherly Love Lodge # 99)
Legacy of Past Master William Holliday
        (As I Knew Him)
P.M. William Holliday, was a humble and
loyal servant of Brotherly Love Lodge # 99.
Although, I have very limited memories of P.M.
Holliday, I did have the chance to meet him
personally, while he was a resident of the
Lake Marion Nursing Facility of Summerton.

One Tuesday night after ① our meeting
was adjourned, we traveled to the nursing
facility. Attending was the (W.M) during that
time, elected officials (S.W.), (J.W), and
other Brethren's. We walk in to the front
desk and ask may we visit P.M. William
Holliday. The receptionist said yes you
may. They went and got P.M. Holliday and
brought him out front where we were anxiously
waiting. Oh, what a night to remember.
Although, he couldn't say anything, but deep
down in my spirit, he knew we were there.
We dressed him as we were dressed with
his P.M. (Hat), (Regallions), black suit and
white shirt. We had a photographer and news
reporter on hand for this Grand Finale'.
We all gather around P.M. Holliday and took
a Brotherly Love Family Portrait). It hit
the news broadcast and made history in
our Grand Lodge for the State of S.C.
This event took place when I (L Joseph James
Jr.) was secretary during the middle ninety's
to the late ninety's.

A year or two later, P.M. Holliday was called
home to be with our Lord. During his last
Rites attend by the Grand Master for the state
of S.C., elected Grand Officials, ⟶

109

Brotherly Love Lodge, Summerton Masonic Lodge, Silver Lodge, and many other Masonic Lodges were all assembled to say (AT Last My Brother.) I shall never forget that Day of Celebration which took place at the Taw Caw Baptist Church of Summerton. OL. What A Home Going Celebration it was for the oldest living Brethern for the State of South Carolina. He was A (Building Block), (Man of Character), (Man of Wisdom), (Man of Faith). He will always be cherished and remembered for the Masonic order for the State of South Carolina. To you, his Grandson, may God forever keep and Bless you for what you're doing in remembrance of your grand Father.

In Closing, I like to leave this thought!

When the Father (Our Lord And Saviour Jesus Christ) meets the Master!

P. M. William Holliday

Written By yours truly"
Brother Joseph Jones Jr.
Secretary (2011)

Submitted by Brother Joseph Jones Jr., Secretary, Brotherly Love Lodge #99

110

John Evans Carter
Remembers Willie Holliday Sr.

Deacon Holliday was like a father to me. He taught me to be a deacon. He had a "gift". When he talked to people they listened. He was upright. Powerful.

He was the church sexton. Every Saturday evening, he had to fill the baptismal pool in the church. And he cleaned the church. He also had to dig the graves. He would walk from his house on 301, through the corn fields, all the way to the church, with the shovel on his back. That is how strong he was.

Deacon Holliday rang the church bell. When a church member died you had to ring the bell three times in the morning. He turned the duty over to me when he got too old. There was a technique to ringing the bell. The church bell is as old as the church and weighs 500 lbs. or more. Just enough force or pressure had to be put on the rope or it had to be pulled in such a way that it did not turn over. If it turned over it could tumble through the floor and the results could be catastrophic.

Deacon Holliday brought me into the lodge. He was a member of 99. I would drive him to Lodge meetings. Deacon Holliday never drove.

Deacon Holliday also took me around to houses and showed me how to give communion. He warned me that some women were fast. He said don't tarry. It could lead to destruction. No kissing on the jaw. Just give the communion and get out. He didn't let nothing wrong go on.

CHAPTER 12

IT STARTS AND ENDS WITH FAMILY

WILLIE HOLLIDAY SR. WITH SONS JOHN, JAMES,
& EDWARD & DAUGHTERS-IN-LAW

Other things may change, but it starts and ends with family.

After 59 years of sharecropping, Willie Holliday Sr. laid down his plow. All he had to show for 59 years of sharecropping was a mountain of debt. Willie had given sharecropping his all but no amount of hard work was going to elevate his quality of life in a system designed for him to fail. U.S. Census records indicate that in 1939 Willie Holliday worked fifty weeks out of the year and earned the pitiful sum of $85.00.

According to Willie's son the late John Holliday, "One could say Willie lived above his means but hardly so! But, sharecropping was a "system of the times".[34] There was always debt at the end of the year and it simply rolled over into the next year's debt.

It wasn't that Willie wasn't ambitious. Willie Holliday Sr. always wanted better. He never stopped dreaming about better and striving to make it happen. Some dreams he talked about and some he didn't. One dream he talked about was getting caught up because he truly believed that one he would get caught up and when he did he was going to build Maggie that big fine house he promised.

---

[34] Claudia Smith Brinson, *Toiling and Thanking God Fills a Long Life.* The State Newspaper. July 13, 2004, 2.

Maggie smiled at the thought. He and Maggie had been married about as long as Willie had been sharecropping and had enjoyed 59 years of wedded bliss. They were still as much in love as the first day they married.

In the late 1940s, Willie Holliday Sr. used his resourcefulness to upgrade the family's lifestyle. He found a way to put electricity in the farmhouse and buy an automobile, an old Ford. Willie Sr. never learned to drive so his son James did most of the driving. When James and Odessa got married and moved to Philadelphia, Odessa remembers Stella writing a letter to James asking him to come back because there was no one to drive the car. The family missed those rides to church on Sunday. Later Brother (Edward's nickname) drove the car. On Sunday mornings, Maggie had to stay on Brother's case to hurry up because he was making her late for church. Willie Holliday Sr., didn't wait for a ride to church. He got dressed and walked from Davis Station to Taw Caw church like he had always done.

By the time Willie Holliday Sr., retired, the children had grown up and most had left South Carolina for the big cities up north like Jersey City, Philadelphia, and Baltimore. Now that Willie was retired, he and Maggie could travel and spend time with the children and their families.

Willie Holliday's grandsons shared memories of his visits.

Rev. Willie Robinson remembers having to give up his room when grandpa came to visit. Karl Holliday remembers grandpa sleeping on the couch at their home in West Philadelphia. Aaron Holliday remembers grandpa sitting on the porch at their home in New Jersey.

3 Generations. Maggie Lee with mother

Maggie & grandsons Mike & Gerard

The Holliday children who settled in Philadelphia were Maggie Lee, John, and James. Maggie Lee lived in Philadelphia only briefly before making her home in Jersey City, New Jersey. There she worked for Maidenform, makers of lingerie, and later she worked at the Standard Laundry on Garfield Avenue. When Maggie's son Boy came to live with her in Jersey City, she got him a job at the Standard Laundry.

John was employed at the Navy Ship Yard in South Philadelphia. The Ship Yard, also known as the "Water Front" was a huge employer in Philadelphia. During World War Two it employed 40,000 people who built 53 ships. A man down on

his luck could show up there on the dock before sunrise, get hired
for day's work, and have money in his pocket by
nightfall

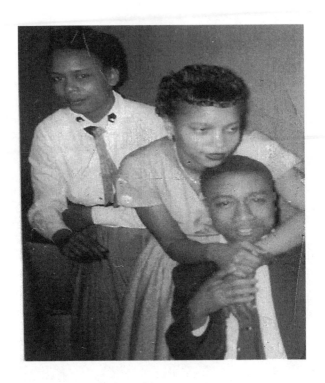

MAGGIE LEE WITH DAUGHTER ETHEL AND A
FRIEND OF ETHEL'S

During the years John worked at the Navy Yard, he helps build two battle ships, the *New Jersey* and the *Wisconsin*. Later John worked as an entrepreneur running a lucrative business called Holliday Beauty Supply in the Philadelphia area.

James Holliday was a construction worker in Philadelphia, employed by the John Keating Company. When James and Odessa first came to Philadelphia, they lived with relatives on Thompson Street in North Philadelphia. Later they bought a home in West Philadelphia where they raised four sons and one daughter.

Willie Holliday Jr. (Buster), Maggie Lee, and Leanese all lived in Jersey City, N.J. Buster worked for his nephew Jim McKnight in the Manufacturing Department of Lester's Hair Products in Jersey City.

Stella, Edward (Brother), and Emma lived in Maryland. Stella's husband and Rev. Robinson's dad, Freddie Robinson, was in charge of Lester's Products Warehouse in Baltimore. Dorothy made her home in South Carolina.

WILLIE HOLLIDAY SR WITH SONS JOHN, JAMES, & EDWARD

Sadly, Maggie Holliday passed away on January 11, 1968. Willie and Maggie had been married for over fifty years and now Willie had to find a way to live without Maggie. It wasn't going to be easy. Willie spent significant time up North with his children and maintained a home in Summerton, South Carolina where he lived alone. James M Knight Jr., remembers coming over to cut his grandfather's hair. When Willie Holliday Sr. was in his 90s and could no longer take care of himself he moved in with a grandson and later with his youngest daughter Dorothy, called Pet, in the Manning/Summerton area of South Carolina. In 1992 he reluctantly entered a nursing home.

Dorothy "Pet" Conyers Remembers Daddy

Youngest Daughter of Willie Holliday Sr.

Daddy's favorite food was fried chicken. He always kept a bag of peppermints and cocoa cola. If you ate without blessing your food he would say, "Yall not going to pray- bless your food. You just going to eat like a bunch of hogs?"

Mom died in January 1968 and he lived alone for one year then went to stay with Roosevelt in Manning. Then he came and stayed with me. I only remember daddy dating one woman after mom died and he said the Lord told him to leave that woman along and go and serve the Lord and he did.

"I never remember daddy drinking. He said he went to a frolic once, long time ago, and woke up in the frost. He told himself he would never drink again and he didn't. Daddy smoked George Washington Tobacco until one night he dreamed he had cancer on

tongue. The next morning, he picked up the pipe, through it in the fire, and never smoked again.

He took BC headache power for headaches and sniffed green alcohol.

When Daddy's Social Security check came he wanted to go to the bank right away. I was still working. He would call me at work and say "come straight home, I have to take care of my business". After I got home and we were driving he got inpatient with the traffic lights. He would say "move light".

Brother Epherm was the oldest. Naomi was the youngest. He said his brother Richard left home and never came back

At the nursing home, Hattie was his nurse and he didn't want her to take care of anyone else.

A month before he died he just slowed down. His hearing was gone, his eyesight went. I saw him that Friday and he was lying in bed on his side. He died Sunday morning about 5:30. He just "went to sleep"."

Willie Holliday, Sr., died on December 19, 2004 at Mariner Healthcare East in Sumter, S.C. He survived five of his ten children and all of his brothers and sisters but one.

Willie Holliday Sr.'s children who preceded him in death are three sons Willie Holliday Jr., James Holliday, Edward Holiday, and two daughters Bertha Holliday Kelly and Maggie Lee Judkins. Willie's one surviving sibling was Naomi Stokes of Cincinnati, Ohio. However, Willie's brother Richard went missing and his date of death remains unknown.

Cynthia McDaniels

Granddaughter of Willie Holliday Sr.

Remembers her grandfather

Grandpa believed in the power of prayer. His nick name "Deak" probably came from "Deacon". He was called nicknamed Bird and Duggar.

Grandpa stayed with Roosevelt and his wife and children in Manning for a couple of years before moving in with us. When he lived with us his bedroom was next door to mine and I would hear him in there talking to someone. He would be talking like someone else was in the room. Well, he was talking to the Lord. He believed in the power of prayer. He would say "don't move until God moves you".

He would put his bed right beside the window and watch the school kids in the morning. He would say, "Better hurry. Bus going to leave you."

He would hit his cane on the floor in the bedroom. I would hear bam, bam, bam. Mom couldn't cook fast enough for him. When mom brought the food in the room, he would say, "Great God. It doesn't take that long to cook food." Then he would want her the door shut and leave the room.

When his check came, we would go to Bi-Lo together. He would tell me to put something in the buggy for myself. That was what he called the shopping cart, the buggy.

Jennifer McKnight

Granddaughter of Willie Holliday

Remembers her Great-Grandfather

What I remember most about grandpa was he liked the ladies…a playboy.

When I was thirteen I helped out at the nursing home. They were like, "Who is your grandfather? That one!!! He likes to flirt with all the nurses". He was a flirt but it wasn't in a creepy way.

He would fuss with my dad, "hope you brought clippers". Dad would say, "But you hardly have hair". Grandpa would say, "I need my head clean for the ladies" (pointing to a patch of hair). I said "you are a hundred and some years old".

When I was about 9 or 10 I would see him at Pet's house. He would come out of the bedroom with that old man's walk. He would pull out a paper bag with some flour in it and fish and start frying. He wouldn't say anything, just frying his fish. He wasn't a hundred years old yet, maybe around 98.

He was in three nursing homes. At the Summerton Nursing Home, he would ask me, "Who are you, Boy's wife?". I would say, "No. Boy's daughter". He would say "Boy's wife. I would respond, "Boy's daughter". This would go on for a minute or two. Then he would chuckle and change the subject. He did every time he saw me. He would say, "You too skinny. These people not feeding you." Then he would holler at the staff, "Yall need to be feeding my granddaughter." They would say, "Willie be quiet". He was always at peace and not sitting around waiting for company. When you came to visit he was like, "You came to visit me. Hi."

I helped out at every nursing home but the last one. I didn't like the last home he was at. It was not like a home....it was too commercial. You go there to see him and they had to look him up in the computer like it was a hospital or something. I don't think he was happy there either, He had to go there because he had lost a lot of his hearing. He would say, "Jesus is done with me". "Just waiting for my body to shut down". My dad would tell him, "You still here because God don't want you".

At his 100th birthday party he was literally surprised by the number of people. He asked, "Who are all these people?" I said,

"These are your people". "My people? Taw Caw?"

By the last nursing home, he knew he was separating from here. He had a deep spirituality. I couldn't be sad. He wasn't sad. He was "letting go".

I respected that man so much. Awesome person. Gosh.

Willie Holliday Sr. with Great-
Great Granddaughter Leasia

CHAPTER 13

Willie Holliday Descendants Who Served Their Country

In Memoriam of Jackie McFarland

- Abram Bowman ARMY-Civil War USCT/Buffalo Soldiers

- Jim McKnight Sr.   USAF   A&E Mechanic

- Jim McKnight Jr.   U.S. Air Force   (See Bio)

- Michael McKnight   U.S. Army   Tech Sgt.

- Patrick Robinson   U.S. Marine

- Patrick Connors

- Willie Holliday, 3rd   U.S. Army

- Jackie McFarland   U.S. Army   Warrant Officer

- Jerome Holliday   U.S. Army   82nd Airborne

- Robert Conyers   U.S. Army

- Aaron Holliday U.S. Navy   1978-1982 USS Dwight D. Eisenhower
- Channing Dandy   U.S. Navy

FAMILY PHOTOS

Children of Willie Holliday's son Edward (Brother)

Jallanar & Michela McKnight

Willie Holliday with Charlotte McKnight and Blaney McKnight

Leasia McKnight

Jeff Davis McFadden

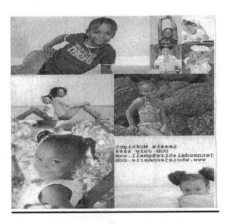

Jenn & Leasia McKnight, Granddaughter
And Great-Granddaughter of Willie Holliday Sr

Jenn & Leasia Mc knight

Children of James and Odessa Holliday

Mike McKnight

Jenn Mc Knight

Maggie Lee with husband and sister "Sank"

MAGGIE LEE HOLLIDAY JUDKINS

CHAPTER 14

FAMILY & FRIENDS REMEMBERS WILLIE HOLLIDAY SR

Angela Robinson-Nutt

Granddaddy was a true man of God. He was a praying grandfather. He was the bell ringer and the sector of Taw Caw Baptist Church. His name is on the cornerstone of the church as one of the first three deacons.

He lived in Camden, New Jersey, with his son, John. In his mid-70s he would travel to South Carolina, Philadelphia, and Baltimore on the Greyhound Bus every year to visit his children, grandchildren, and great-grandchildren. I remember dentures and a hearing aid but very little wrinkles.

At the age of 80 his children, family and friends all gathered to celebrate his birthday. On his 100th birthday, 5 generations were represented. He was still able to call his children and grandchildren by name. Born in 1894, he went home to be with the Lord at the age of 110. Some say 111.

Johnnie E. Holliday (Grandson):

Grandpa would say, "You my oldest grandchild by my oldest child and every time I see you I want my $5.00.

Aaron Holliday (Grandson):

Here's a story that shows just how smart grandpa was.

When I was about 13 or 14 years old, there were three young ladies that lived up the street from me between the ages of 24 and 26. They were stunningly beautiful women and quite intimidating to your teenage boys. Whenever my friends and I would see them we would attempt to say something smooth and cool jut to get their attention. Looking back on it they were probably thinking 'awwww, how cute.' Anyway one day I was coming home from school just before summer recess and to my surprise there was one of the young ladies on the porch relaxing on the glide rocker talking up a storm with grandpa, I was stunned. Not only was this beautiful woman chillin on our porch she actually spoke to me. Grandpa said "say something boy", again I froze for a few seconds (I wasn't ready LOL) but was able to at least say hi eventually. About an hour later after I finished my chores I went back outside hoping to get another eyeful of this beautiful woman, unfortunately by the time I returned she was gone. I sat down next to grandpa and said to him "how do you do it, it doesn't seem to matter who it is somehow you are always able to get perfect strangers to stop and spend time with you, how do you do it? What he said to me would change how I saw myself and how I interacted with others, this is what he said, "I can be me all day long." I have to admit that at the time I had o clue what he meant by that, but as I grew older I was able to understand the meaning and wisdom of this words. What he was telling me was that all he was doing was being himself. Unlike most people when you met our grandfather what you were getting was the real McCoy, there was nothing fake about him. With him it was what you see is what you get. He told me he was comfortable in his own skin, he said "I may be a little older and a little wiser but I am still me and that is enough. Just being me allows others to relax and gives them permission to do the same".

This is some of the best advice that I have ever received and its something that I live by to this day

Mike McKnight (Great-Grandson):

My name is Michael McKnight. I can remember grandpa coming to stay with us in Jersey City sometimes. We had so much fun giving him a haircut. I always felt it was something special about him. He always read he bible. I felt really proud after becoming a Prince Hall Freemason and I shook his hand while visiting him with my father. He was

at the home in Sumter, SC. I think he was about 110 years old then. I still remember the expression on his face when I gave him the handshake. I always saw him as an upright man while growing up. I will always keep fond memories of him.

Bert Stukes Johnson

When the church members would be to the nursing home to give him communion, he would say "One more time. Thank you Lord for one more time."

George McDaniels

He was an on-time. He meant 8:00 not 8:01.

Esther Carter

I knew Deacon Holliday and his wife Maggie. She was a pretty lady. Nice. I remember all of us walking to Watch Night Service by Moonlight.

Sonny Richburg

I remember Mr. Holliday moving from one side of the road to the other. He worked for Touchberry Farms. Once he traded cows with my father. I don't know why they traded cows except maybe he liked that cow better.

Leanese "Sank" Shuler (Daughter, living):

"Get out there & get in that field". "Yellin' Daddy." "Strict, no boyfriends."

Ben Holliday

I was about 11, 12, or younger. I would describe granddaddy as "Flirtatious". His nickname as "Dugar".

Karl Holliday (Grandson)

Prayer was important to Grandpa. Prayer through faith for whatever obstacle. He just like to go to church. I was intimidated by him because he was strict. He had a strong work ethic. Didn't matter how much money you made, just work. He loved his family. "That's all you got".

Rodney L. Holliday (Grandson)

Account Executive with Philadelphia Tribune Newspaper-- The nation's oldest continually published Black newspaper. Father of three.

My remembrance of him was making a way out of no way as in travel in Philadelphia with his suitcase fastened with neckties.

Iota Holliday (Uncle John's Wife

Thanks for reaching out to me concerning "Dad's legacy. He was your grandfather and I married his fourth child, John W. Holliiday, Sr., therefore I refer to him as "Dad". I was in awe when I met him in 1989. First, after talking to him for a few minutes, I knew that he was a God-fearing man and strong in his belief in our Lord & Savior Jesus Christ. I know without a doubt that his children were raised to fear God and I was privileged and blessed to have met John. I could be lengthy in my input, but will end by saying that I am blessed and thankful to be a part of the Holliday Family (forever, until I see Jesus) ...

JULLANAR MCKNIGHT

The most memorable moment I have of Great-great grandpa Holliday is the time I attended his 100th birthday party in South Carolina. I was amazed that he was standing and walking on his own. I watched him eat his food with no help and when people tried to help he rejected their assistance. That was empowering to me.

Children of Willie and Maggie McFadden-Holliday

Bertha Holliday Kelly "Nonie"

Mother of one daughter, Lillie

Maggie Lee Holliday-Judkins

(Lee)

1921-1965

Mother of Two Children James & Ethel

James E. Mc Knight, Sr. ("Boy")

James Jr	Michael	Gerrard	Jennifer
Jamere	Michela	Ayanna	Leasia
Jullanar		Jabari	Alex
Jasaad		Darryl (D)	Kaz
Fatimah			Aurora
Feheem			

Ethel McKnight Privott

Arnie	Germaine	Clevie	Tracy	Truzell
Kenitra	Jack	1 Unknown	Lucy	Tariq
Sharona	Missy			Triston
Aurell	Kiauntee			Shytera
1 Unknown	Elysha			Trent

Willie Holliday, Jr. (Buster)

8/9/1922 – 4/13/1983

Children

Johnnie

Willie

Elijah

Vevelyn

Benjamin James Holliday

Doris Ann Holliday-Winston

Patricia Dean Holliday-Halley

Grandchildren

Yolanda holliday

Theatis Halley

Thyson Halley

Anesia Halliday

Great-Grandchildren

Sheniqua Holliday

Keyshawn Holliday

Teshirah Halley

Thyqall Holliday

John W. Holliday

3/30/1924-9/26/2013

Children   **Grandchildren**

Beverly (D)

Saretta

John, Jr.

Sheila

Aaron

Erron

Antoine

Cherron

James Holliday

1929-3/29/79

Children

John Henry	**Angela**
Jerome (d)	**Rodney**
Gregory	
Karl	

James Holliday (continue)

Grandchildren

Anthony Jones	Samir Holliday
Kia Wise	Felicia Holliday
Eugene	Latoyia Norman
Tremaine	Felicia Holliday
Rasheed Wise	Arionne Buckner
Naimah Holliday	D'janah Holliday
Madinah Holliday	Heaven Holliday
Laqreshia Norman	Serenity Holliday

Great-Grandchildren

Eunique	Raliegh	Canyah
Nasir	Ryan	Chanya
Malik		Chanelle
Tremell		Ciahnni Norman
Khalif		Caliyah
Ojhanay Wise		Zair Jones

Stella Holliday Robinson (Duke)

10/13/31 – 9/10/2015

Children

Rev.-Dr. Willie E. Robinson

Delores Cherry

Magdeline Shearin

Freda Bennett

Angela Robinson-Nutt

Grandchildren

Patrick

Jermaine

Stella Robinson (Continue)

Lanice
Alisha

Melissa
Shawna

8 great-grandchildren

Emma Jane Holliday-Oliver (Bird/Mama/Biggy)

(7/3/1933-9/10/2013)

Children

Tony, Jr.	Delores	Sammy (D)
Dorothy	Donald	Tyrone (D)
Evon	Jeanette	John
Henry	Suzanne	Patricia

Edward Holiday ("Brother")

(4/17/36-12/24/2001)

Children

Vermell	Jennifer
Vernette	Rex
Kathy	Clarence

Edward Holliday (continue)

Grandchildren

Taneka	Kayla
Ebony	Christopher
Dierra	Janae
Rex, Jr.	Nehemiah
Michael III	Keyanna
Shae	Shanekia

Latrin

Leanese Holliday Shuler (Sank)

<u>Children</u>

Grinett

Denise

Robert

Shirley

Barbara Anne

Renee Williams

Harold

Sandy

Donna

Charles

Adrianne

22 Grandchildren, 10 great-grandchildren

Dorothy Conyers (Pet)

Children

Roosevelt   Jackie

Richard   Cynthia McDaniel

Bobby (D)

Grandchildren

Takisha Rowzee   Terrence McDaniel

Great-Grandchildren

Jordyn Sanders   Jaleah Rowzee

Accomplishments

James McKnight Jr.

- **B.S. in Business Administration- Strayer University**
- **Retired- U.S. Air Force -Master Sergeant**
- **20 years experience in Logistics Management**
- **The Meritorious Service Medal**
- **Currently employed by Army -Dept. of Defense – 12 years**

Michael Mc Knight

- **B.A. University of Maryland**
- **Retired SFC U.S. Army – Honorable Discharge**
- **Served in both Iraq wars and in 2 wa zones, Middle East & Balkans**
- **Current- Emergency Manager**

Gerard Mc Knight with daughter Ayanna& niece

Michela

- **Graduated, B.S. Accounting, Virginia Commonwealth Univ., 1997**
- **Founded/Established GDM Accounting & Tax Service, 1992**
- **Active in High School Sports –High Jump Record, 1982**
- **All Conference High School Football Team, State Championship**
- **Tax Enrolled Agent, Internal Revenue**
- **Featured in Black Enterprise Magazine Article, "Beware of Bad Tax Advice".**

FATIMAH MC KNIGHT

- **Salisbury University**
- **B.A. in Communications-Media Production**
- **Employed in Telecommunications-Engineering Firm**

MICHELA MC KNIGHT

- **Master's Degree in Foreign Languages for Commerce with ability to speak English, German, Italian, French, and Spanish.**
- **Controlling/Operational Efficiency Manager in the International Steel Industry.**
- **Fully accomplished Lyricist, Singer, Musician**
- **Web Designer**

Ayanna McKnight

- **Virginia Commonwealth University: Major- Homeland Security, Minor, Russian Studies**
- **Graduated from Clover Hill High School**
- **Intern through Richmond office of Emergency Management**

Nekaiya Jacobs

- **Pediatric Intensive Care Physician at University of Florida**
- **Studied at University of South Carolina**

Jerome Holliday (1950-2009)

- **Graduate, Temple University**
- **Drug Addiction Supervisor & Counselor**
- **Employee of the Year**

Karl Holliday

- **Graduate High School 1976**
- **Self-made Businessman**
- **Married, father of two**

Leasia McKnight

- **Class of 2018**
- **Tacoma School of the Arts**
- **3.4 GPA**
- **Internship at Anderson Island Elementary**
  Teaching music and Ukulele
- **Pursuing Music Therapy**
- **Planning to attend Berklee College of Music**

Alex Payne

- **Applied for and attended Seabury**
- **Showed interest and visited MIT this past summer**
- **Completed University of Washington Summer Program for Math**

Serenity A. Holliday

- Graduated, Pennwood High School
- Member of Track Team
- Freshman, Indiana University

Jullanar McKnight

- **Licensed Cosmetologist in Maryland**
- **Certified Texture expert and hair therapist**
- **Owner and founder of Lana Fierce Salon and Lana Fierce Collection**

In Memoriam of Daryl Christopher Devlin

Darryl loved everyone and everyone loved him and his music

May 10, 1984 – January 3, 201

Book for All Americans: History, Education, & Knowledge

Harold and Freddie Wilcox and Jim McKnight aka Holliday until age 15

Jim McKnight a/k/a "Boy Holliday"

My reason for writing this book is for the purpose of maintaining a permanent history of my grandfather, Willie Holliday, Sr.'s life and 112 years of activities, for his current and future descendants, to educate, show, and tell examples.

A family tree up through grandchildren and great-grandchildren (as available) will be an integral part of the story, which will allow them to continue the tree as interested. For the past 25 years before Grandpa's death, his descendants had the privilege of visiting him on his birthday gatherings and getting to know him, whereas his future descendants and family friends will not have such a privilege. His legend will in this book which will live on and be known by future youth descendants, and serves the purpose of identifying "kinfolks", as in the language of grandpa. This family tree will enable them to do such.

In this book my plans are to point out and tell his story. I am drawing from the memories, comments, and experiences from as many of his family and friends as possible, as well as press releases and photos. My genealogist, Sahara Bowser was instrumental in tracing my grandfather's family tree back to 1810.

I am Willie Holliday Sr.'s grandson who used his last name Holliday as my last name until age 16 of which he raised me from age 3. He also gave me the nickname "Boy". I went to School District One, Scotts Branch Elementary & High School. I attended St. Peter's College, Jersey City, N.J., and as a student I founded the Inner City Business Project (ICBT), a project believed to be the first in the country to assist minority and female entrepreneurs under the Urban Studies Department. The ICBT was nationally televised on ABC's The Christopher Hour for two years.

Among my other achievements and accomplishments are

Consultant to the Clarendon County in developing a program as part of the First Stripped Bass Festival in the county, the birthplace of Briggs v Board in School District One, and the Supreme Court Decision on Brown v Board (read Simple Justice by Author Richard Kluger). As a part of the First Stripped Bass Festival, establish a program to honor the original complaints signature roster of 21 signers, and had a cornerstone installed by me and staff with the Prince Hall Grand Lodge in front of the school on the lawn, and the original 21 were honored by being awarded a signed copy of Simple Justice by author

Richard Kluger at the ceremony held at Scott's Branch Middle School in Summerton. In addition to research and developing a listing of all Black Historical Achievements in the County.

Partial Listing of other Consultant Assignments

- Establishment of Summerton's first Medical Clinic

- Taw Caw Little League -the first Official Little League in Clarendon, County

- Small Farm Assistance -Clarendon County Pea Project (Lord Chesterfield's Pea Project

- Quest Boat Builders

- The We Academy

   STARS (Sandhills Theater Arts Renaissance School), Southern Pines, NC

- No Grease Barbering School of Tonnuling – dedicated to educating ex-offenders into barbering industry

Lecturing and Business Development in various African and South American Countries

- International Marketing in several Countries

- Lectured in several African and South American Countries

- Developed and taught a small business class at Central Piedmont in Charlotte, NC.

,

This book is written for the current and future youth, especially the ones from Summerton and the Clarendon County, South Carolina, area.

As a 7-year-old child, I was fortunate to meet the Wilcox family (see photo) who lived two miles from my grandfather in a log cabin. They were kind enough to allow me to play with their kids my age (see photo) and eventually paid me a few dollars to cut the grass, which led to other chores, such as fishing guide, with the future eventuality of being given left over food from their very important guest events. I am at a lost of words as to how to explain how worthy that was to the Holliday family as our menus were often limited to cornbread and cabbage. There is a humanitarian element in the Mr. Wilcox who gave me my first opportunity as a grass cutting entrepreneur. Little was it known that my efforts with the Wilcox were to escape the cotton fields at an early age.

The slavery of sharecropping which never allowed Grandpa the opportunity to buy his house as he talked about due to never obtaining a profit in over fifty years is real. However, under the circumstances he was able to raise 10 plus 1.

At 5 years old my pet dog got rabies and I was attacked by him in the sweet potato field. Grandpa rushed me to save me and prepared the mule and wagon to take me to the Summerton Drug Store where Dr. Gordon started a series of shots, of which I had to walk 2 miles each morning to get before school ad then a half mile future to school. This was repeated for 21 consecutive days and I could not be late for school. The shots put a lasting fear of needles in me.

My schooling at Scotts Branch School was a fun time for me as it was an escape from the cotton fields and I was able to establish new friends which was limited where we lived (where the old Federal Mogul Plant sit) on 301 across from the new school. At age 6 -7 I got diphtheria (swollen throat) from kerosene and had to receive 3 shots one each day. Shots were not my thing. Thanks daddy (I called Grandpa daddy) for the mule and wagon vehicle to and from the doctor in Summerton.

My being the first grandchild of Willie Holliday. Sr., to graduate from college with a degree, I owe my thanks and respect to him and I feel obligated to tell his history. I am indebted to him for getting me started in life, as he did with so many despite his living conditions.

James E. McKnight, formerly known as James "Boy" Holliday

Jim McKnight Launched Lester
Hair Products

TAW CAW LITTLE LEAGUE NEWS ARTICLES, LETTERS, AND PHOTOS

Caw Little League
stration to be held

Taw Caw Little League
adds new age levels

The Taw Caw Church Winner team at Shoney's Sayville Rest Area.

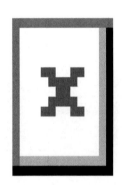

Taw Caw Little League All Stars (Top photo)

Shaw AFB Team (Bottom photo)

Safety Officer

Lester's (Jim McKnight) in Zaire

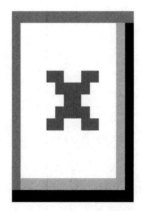

Jim McKnight with Children in Africa

Epilogue

Summerton, 2017

The town of Summerton, South Carolina, Willie Holliday Sr.'s town, has not changed much at all since he passed away in 2004.

The homes, the Sharecropper's shacks, Willie Holliday Sr. lived in are gone and the fields where Willie Holliday toiled are overgrown with weeds. The Federal Mogul Plant site is built over one of the homes. But the town of Summerton still looks like it did in Willie Holliday's time. Summerton doesn't have a supermarket and the medical center it had once has closed down.

Willie's school, Scott's Branch, built on the blood, sweat, and tears of his parents during Reconstruction still exist in its

1930's location on 4th Street. Time have forgotten that Scott's Branch was originally the Taw Caw School started at the Taw Caw Baptist Church during Reconstruction. It is one of few original black schools that came out of Reconstruction era that still exist. The brook named Scott's Branch that ran behind the gin house school has dried up. There is an opening in the ground where the brook used to run.

A cornerstone honoring the 21 petitioners of Briggs vs Board is prominently displayed on the lawn of the middle school. It was installed at the First Stripped Bass Festival.

Jim Mc Knight stands at plaque
honoring 21 petitioners of Briggs
(Brown) vs Board

The Taw Caw Little League has been dissolved. It was an
Official Chartered International Little League that originated in
Summerton. In its first historic season the Taw Caw Little League

came in third best in the State of South Carolina.

A subsequent visit to Summerton presented an opportunity to visit the impressive Taw Caw Center, a state-of-the-art center at Taw Caw Missionary Baptist, the church Willie Holliday Sr. attended all his life. The center contains a basketball court that converts to a banquet room, a modern top-of-the-line kitchen, and a computer lab. The center can be used as an emergency center and has been used as an emergency shelter in the past.

The Taw Caw church where Willie Holliday Sr. served as church sexton and deacon is still going strong under the leadership of Rev. William Johnson. Surely, Willie Holliday Sr., in in heaven singing his praises.

Bibliography

Altman, Susan. "Black Architects Have a Rich American History." *The Encyclopedia of African-American Heritage*, 1997.

Ancestry.com. U.S. Census Records

Bennett, Sonia. "Sharecropping and Tenant Farming." UXL Encyclopedia of U.S. History. Last modified 2009.

Brinson, Claudia S. "Toiling and Thanking God Fills a Long Life." *The State Newspaper*(Manning), July 13, 2004, 2.

FamilysearchOrg. U.S. Census Records

Kluger, Richard. *Simple Justice: The History of Brown V. Board of Education and Black America's Struggle for Equality.* New York, NY: Knopf Doubleday Publishing Group, 2011.

McKnight, Jim. "It Was a Different Time for 109-year-old Clarendon Man." *Times Extra*(Manning), July 13, 2004, 3.

New Orleans Delta. "Negroes and Cotton." *Southern Cultivator*, 1859, 282.

Phillips, Kenneth E. "Sharecropping and Tenant Farmer in Alabama." *Encyclopedia of Alabama*, April 24, 2015.

Scottsbranchhighschoolalumni.com. "Scott's branch high school." Sbhaa. Last modified 2012.

Vaughn, Emily. "Carolina Pearson-Johnson." *Blacks Establish Town of Summerton* (blog). 2008. emilyvaugh.com.

White House Historical Association. WHHA. Accessed November 12, 2017. http://whitehousehistory.org.

Wikipedia Contributors. "Grits." The Free Wikipedia. n.d. http://en.wikipedia.org.

ABOUT THE AUTHOR

Author Sahara Bowser with Richard Stewart, owner of
Pocahontas Black History Museum, Petersburg, Virginia

Other Titles by Sahara Bowser

- Candy in the Sand
- What Jael Did (God's Diva Jael)
- Dancing Naked (Salome from New Testament)
- God's Diva Jael Bible Study Book
- Don't Sweep Dirt Out the Door After Dark
- Chillin' in the Rose Garden on a Jazzy Afternoon